PARENTING ADHD KIDS SIMPLIFIED

THE ESSENTIAL GUIDE FOR EFFECTIVE BEHAVIOR MANAGEMENT, EMPOWERED ACADEMIC SUCCESS, AND IMPROVED FAMILY HARMONY

LUCY MARVAR

CONTENTS

INTRODUCTION

 *Never be afraid to travel on a new path.*

— LAILAH GIFTY AKITA

It was the most beautiful sound I've ever heard—a symphony at birth that only a parent can appreciate—that first wail. That was my situation; however, it is not just limited to birth. Fostering and adoption ... well, we all have the same front row.

Alas, I had the whole parenting gig figured out! Of course, I did; we all do—upbringing, education, sports, you name it—all perfectly mapped out, right? I just wanted the best, as I aimed for the stars! However, it seems like someone had plans of their own. Let me call them quirks. Yes, quirks. Extracurricular activities? School? Birthday parties and social interactions? It was like navigating a minefield of interesting social encounters and fleeting attention spans. Worst of all, nothing worked, no matter how much I tried to explain, scold, and warn. Why is my kid not normal? Do other parents have some secret manual for this? Am I failing as a parent?

While wondering and wishing for my child to be "normal," I simultaneously embarked on a quest to improve my parenting. The issue may have been with me all along. So, I introduced a range of activities, hoping that something might stick; however, it was useless. I was at a loss. After all, no instructions come with them when they're born. Frustration, stress, and anxiety slowly started setting in. I couldn't grasp the obliviousness; it seemed like my kid was living in a different world. It felt like a locked door between us, and I didn't have the right key to open it and adequately connect with my child.

That's it; I hit a wall, and it was time to call in the professionals. It was then that the verdict came in: my child was diagnosed with attention deficit hyperactivity disorder (ADHD). Say what? Is this a tongue twister of some sort? It turns out that ADHD is a relatively common neurobiological disorder that affects between 3%–11% of children, which leads to 30%–50% of child referrals for mental health services (Strahm, 2020). Do hyperactivity, impulsivity, diminished attention span, and somewhat quirky behaviors ring bells? However, what about you? Are confusion, frustration, perhaps anxiety, guilt, and feelings of hopelessness ringing any bells? Where does this diagnosis leave us as parents?

Well, it's a laundry list that stretches far beyond. There's the self-doubt, academic concerns, parent-child challenges, and feelings of isolation. Then, we have the physical daily struggles to navigate as well; think sibling relationships, medication management, and advocating for support and understanding. And, the most challenging thing: seeing your child suffer and grapple with the challenges of navigating life with ADHD. But let's take one collective breath because the world is a multi-faceted place filled with wonder. Not everything is wired the same and can fit into the standard mold that's often presented. I am intimately familiar with this journey. I also understand that there comes a point where, as a parent, you seek something more. It is something powerful yet straightforward, especially when grappling with the added complexities that come with ADHD. We know there's no cure, but we, as parents, hold the power to enhance the quality of life for everyone involved in this diagnosis dynamic.

The solution? It's relatively simple: learn how to manage the symptoms and provide the necessary support properly. And here, in your hands, you hold a wealth of information that will provide you with simple yet highly effective strategies to navigate this journey. Think of them as practical shortcuts. Together, we will cover everything! From the symptoms, diagnosis process, and proven techniques to behavior and emotional management. But it doesn't end there; we will delve into some insights on improving social skills in various settings—whether school, family, or friends. This knowledge encapsulates every aspect that will contribute to a more fulfilled life and a promising future for your child. And you can be sure these benefits will spill over into your life, significantly alleviating stress and anxiety and boosting your confidence as a parent!

I do want to emphasize that my understanding comes not only from being a parent of three, one of whom has been diagnosed with ADHD, but also from being a registered nurse. I know all about it, from diagnosis to signs and symptoms, different types, statistics, myths, and different age groups to what it takes for your child to uncover their prosperity. Yes, I have fully immersed myself. Thus, from a perspective of knowledge and firsthand experience, I'm well-versed in what it takes for your child to step into their version of success. I wish to share this knowledge because every parent and child navigating this journey deserves the best. And trust me, it's entirely possible.

Thus, let's take that first step together and understand the truth behind ADHD.

1

UNDERSTANDING THE TRUTH ABOUT ADHD

> *Start each day with a positive thought and a grateful heart.*
>
> — ROY T. BENNETT

It's the morning rush, and you are diligently juggling the madness like a pro. You prepped the lunchboxes and ensured everyone was dressed. You even ensured you were dressed and ready for the onslaught of a new day.

You sit down at the breakfast table, and suddenly, cereal takes flight through the air, milk cascades onto the floor, and you watch slowly as the bowl swirls across the tiles. Nevertheless, things do not end there. Your toddler breaks down into uncontrollable sobs as your phone starts chiming in. Your attempt at figuring out how to soothe your toddler, clean up the mess, and reach the phone ignites a surge of overwhelm. It's all part of the grand circus. Ah, the beautiful unpredictability of parenting. It's sometimes akin to a high-wire act of juggling flaming torches on a unicycle! I understand that every day is different; sometimes, it feels like we need more than just one crayon from the box. However, what if I shared a hack with you?

PAUSE FOR PARENTS: POSITIVE AFFIRMATIONS

There is a wondrous way to reframe your thinking that will prevent you from internalizing setbacks, such as bad grades and meltdowns, as a personal reflection on you as a person and parent.

I'm referring to positive affirmations. These positively charged statements put a lid on that nagging inner critic. You know, the inner voice that floods the mind with doubts and negative self-talk. Positive affirmations ignite more positive thought patterns, curb stress and anxiety, boost confidence, and foster a stronger sense of self. Positive affirmations are more than wishful thinking; it is a mental gym session for your brain. After all, we spend so much time improving our physical health, why not do the same for the brain? These positive mental repetitions reprogram your thinking, giving your mind a new script.

Moreover, you will begin to think and act differently with consistent practice. This affirmation is not just my take; it is rooted in the self-affirmation theory! This theory suggests that we as humans are motivated to protect ourselves from threats by painting self-integrity, and by saying positive things about ourselves, we can help ourselves feel better about who we are (Steele, 1988).

Now, do not misunderstand; positive affirmations are not a magical overnight cure for anxiety and self-doubt. However, practicing regularly and consistently can shift how you perceive yourself and interpret your experiences. It does sound simple, and it is!

It's a beautiful scenario of minimum input, with consistency, of course, and maximum benefit. Why not give it a try?

Pick one positive affirmation that aligns with your values to repeat throughout the day. Let us look at a couple of ideas to get the ball rolling:

- I'm a good parent. I got this.
- My children thrive because of my parenting abilities.
- I'm a resilient parent.
- I'm a good listener.
- Parenting comes very naturally to me.
- I put my heart into everything I do.
- I show up and am fully present for my family every day.
- I trust my parenting abilities and instincts.
- It's okay to take care of myself.
- It's okay to ask for and accept help.

THE MYTHS AND MISCONCEPTIONS OF ADHD

Knowledge is compelling, but unfortunately, when it comes to ADHD, there is a lot of misinformation, labels, and assumptions out there. Let us clear the air around some of these fallacies.

My Child Is Too Young to Have ADHD

ADHD is not exclusive to school-aged children; symptoms and diagnoses can manifest during preschool years as well. At times, even a doctor has difficulty recognizing the difference between expected behavior in preschool versus ADHD behavior. When a preschooler's functioning and developmental behavior significantly interfere with life, it causes disruption. At this point, an ADHD diagnosis aims to assess the intensity of these behaviors.

They Are Just Lazy

This label is a rather tough one to digest and, strangely enough, one of the most common misconceptions! Challenges in functioning development may appear as a lack of motivation, such as difficulty completing tasks, sitting still, or staying focused; these challenges require proper support to bridge them.

They're a Handful

ADHD is a functional disability that these young children struggle with daily. They're not a handful of daydreamers; they suffer in a society that misunderstands their challenges across all aspects of their lives.

There Is a Cure

No cure or magic pill will make ADHD disappear. It's a chronic condition and often requires treatment changes, including medications, to navigate life at different developmental stages.

They Can Focus, So They Do Not Have ADHD

If a child plays games for extended periods of time, it doesn't negate the presence of ADHD at all. Challenges with ADHD are complex, not just about focus but also about organization and sustained effort.

It's Just Poor Parenting

ADHD is certainly not a result of poor parenting. However, it is duly that poor parental discipline can amplify ADHD-related symptoms, just as effective parenting can help regulate and effectively manage them.

They Will Outgrow It

Unfortunately, that is not true; ADHD persists into adulthood. While there is improvement, ADHD will always be required to facilitate changes for a fully productive adult life.

It's Not a Real Condition

ADHD is an actual condition recognized by the National Institutes of Health, CDC, and American Psychiatric Association as a difference in brain development.

ADHD Kids Are All Hyperactive

Not all children diagnosed with ADHD exhibit hyperactivity as a symptom. There are different types of ADHD, one of which does not impact activity levels.

It's a Learning Disability

ADHD is not a learning disability; however, symptoms may negatively impact learning. Conversely, specific learning disabilities often co-occur with ADHD.

The Dangers of ADHD Stigma

Stigmas have a dark side attached to them, compounding the challenges of dealing with an ADHD diagnosis. It's genuinely something that warrants more attention in society, emphasizing the importance of not only understanding but also embracing neuro-diversity.

The stigma around ADHD for those grappling with the condition is not reserved. It also affects parents and other family members. Assumptions such as impulsive behaviors reflect poor parenting and are a standard label. But here is a little secret: your child's ADHD diagnosis does not mirror your parenting quality. Anyone can get diagnosed with ADHD for various reasons. Thankfully, there are plenty of measures parents can take to mitigate symptoms and navigate the ADHD journey with greater ease. The stigma saga does not end here. It even extends to girls and minorities. Black, Asian, Pacific Islander, and Latino children are less likely to be diagnosed with ADHD and receive the appropriate medication and treatment. However, again, there are various reasons for this, including the perception that it's a disciplinary issue, parental failure, and a general distrust in the medical community. Girls, in general, are not as rowdy compared to boys and are also more likely to internalize and blame themselves when they go through tough times. This stigma only contributes to an onslaught of additional problems, such as depression, anxiety, and eating disorders. These factors make it even harder to diagnose girls as having ADHD, resulting in delayed diagnoses and treatment.

Irrespective of race, religion, or gender, stigma sticks and negatively impacts anyone, giving rise to a host of additional challenges. The health and well-being of children and family members come under fire, manifesting in various ways. Low self-esteem, depression, anxiety, disruptive sleep, substance abuse, and bullying may all be possible results of stigmatization. These additional challenges make it even harder for a child already dealing with challenges coupled with ADHD. Unfortunately, the impacts of stigma may persist into adulthood.

To best ward against the negative impacts of stigma, offering support, advocating, and raising awareness, along with maintaining a positive attitude, can provide solace and help those struggling with ADHD thrive.

WHAT ADHD IS

What is the difference between attention deficit disorder (ADD) and attention deficit hyperactivity disorder (ADHD)? There is no difference; ADD is merely a "vintage" term that transitioned to ADHD in 1987 by simply adding the term "hyperactivity" to the mix.

Now that we have cleared that all up, what exactly is ADHD? It's one of the most common neurodevelopmental disorders diagnosed in children, lasting into adulthood. There is no cure; it can only be treated and managed. Associated with impulsive behaviors, difficulty paying attention, and hyperactivity, ADHD presents itself in three different ways: predominantly inattentive presentation, predominantly hyperactive-impulsive presentation, and combined presentation. It's important to note that ADHD symptoms may change over time; the presentation of ADHD may also change. ADHD diagnosis is determined according to which types of symptoms are more prevalent. Let us hone in on each of these presentations for a better understanding.

Predominantly Inattentive Presentation

- Challenges in organization
- Difficulties with completing tasks
- Lack of attention to details
- Difficulties following instructions or conversations
- Easily distracted

- Forgetfulness regarding daily routine details

Predominantly Hyperactive-Impulsive Presentation

- Excessive fidgeting
- Excessive talking
- Unable to remain seated for extended periods
- Impulsivity
- Restlessness
- Excessive running, climbing, or jumping in younger children
- Speaking out of turn
- Interrupting conversations
- Inability to wait their turn
- Difficulty in listening to instructions/directions
- Accident prone

Combined Presentation

- Symptoms of predominantly inattentive presentation and predominantly hyperactive-impulsive presentation are present simultaneously.

HOW PREVALENT IS ADHD?

Let us talk numbers and look into some statistics that will offer valuable insight into the prevalence of ADHD:

- Approximately 265,000 children in the United States, aged between 3 and 5 years, have been diagnosed with ADHD (Centers for Disease Control and Prevention, 2022b).
- Approximately 2.4 million children in the United States, aged between 6 and 11 years, have been diagnosed with

ADHD (Centers for Disease Control and Prevention, 2022b).

- Approximately 3.3 million children in the United States, aged between 12 and 17 years, have been diagnosed with ADHD (Centers for Disease Control and Prevention, 2022b).
- Approximately 129 million children in the United States, aged between 5 and 19 years, have been diagnosed with ADHD (CHADD, 2018c).
- Approximately 9.8% (nearly 6 million) of children in the United States, aged between 3 and 17 years, have received an ADHD diagnosis at some point, compared to 8.7% (over 5 million) of U.S. children with a current ADHD diagnosis (Bitsko et al., 2022).
- Approximately 35% to 78% of children with an ADHD diagnosis maintain symptoms as an adult (Schein et al., 2022).
- Approximately 2.6% (equivalent to 139.8 million) of adults worldwide experienced persistent ADHD from childhood, which includes individuals who experienced childhood onset paired with ADHD symptoms that continued into adulthood (Song et al., 2021).
- The prevalence of worldwide symptomatic adult ADHD declines with age: 18- to 24-year-olds account for over 75.5 million cases, whereas individuals over 60 contribute to approximately a total of 46.4 million cases (Song et al., 2021).

POTENTIAL CAUSES OF ADHD

A specific cause does not precisely narrow down the origin of ADHD. Nonetheless, it may develop from a combination of environmental and genetic factors. For now, let us take a look at a few potential factors, including brain development, trauma, and prenatal factors, which may come into play in the causation of ADHD.

Brain Development

ADHD does not only cause changes in the brain but is also suspected to arise from changes happening to and in the brain, such as brain structure, brain chemistry, brain function, and brain injuries. Let us pop on some lab coats and delve right in!

Brain Structure

A neuroimaging study conducted in 2017 discovered that specific brain regions and overall brain volume were smaller in study participants with ADHD compared to study participants without ADHD (Hoogman et al., 2017). The theory that ADHD causes developmental delays in various brain regions supported the fact that these discrepancies in brain volume were a whole lot more noticeable in children with ADHD compared to adults.

The brain regions explored during this neuroimaging study included the following:

- The nucleus accumbens is involved in reward processing.
- The hippocampus is involved in emotion and motivation.
- The amygdala influences emotional regulation.
- The caudate nucleus and putamen coordinate smooth movement.

Brain Chemistry

As the name implies brain chemistry is all about the chemicals in the brain that impact the nervous system and influence mood. There are various chemicals, and one significant one is the "happy hormone" dopamine, which is responsible for fueling motivation, the drive for reward, and the experience of pleasure. However, it's not just about fun with dopamine; it also plays a crucial role in focus, memory, executive, and motor functions. A 2009 study uncovered an unfortunate truth: individuals with ADHD have lower dopamine levels compared to those without ADHD (Volkow et al., 2009). Some suggest that this reduction of dopamine is caused by higher concentrations of dopamine transporters (proteins) in the brains of people with ADHD. Lower dopamine levels could cause dissatisfaction, unhappiness, and boredom if not managed. However, it's essential to note that the lines are still blurred when it comes to the relationship between ADHD and dopamine.

Brain Function

A review from a study conducted using functional MRI found that individuals diagnosed with ADHD noted differences in brain networks that are associated with reward processing (Rubia, 2018). In the same study, they also discovered that people with ADHD may experience impairment challenges in various brain networks that govern essential functions, such as cognitive control, working memory, attention, and timing. As an example, children diagnosed with ADHD have decreased activation in brain regions when they are engaged in tasks that involve decision-making and rewards.

Brain Injury

A traumatic brain injury (TBI) is an injury to the brain that is so severe that it affects how the brain functions. Research on overnight TBI hospitalizations of children between the ages of three and seven found that there is a strong correlation between these types of injuries and ADHD, leaving children who experienced a TBI more susceptible to ADHD for up to seven years post-injury (Narad et al., 2018). Up to 62% of the children participating in the study later developed ADHD, also referred to as secondary ADHD.

Trauma

Let us cross over to psychological trauma, which refers to a physical or emotional response triggered by a highly distressing event.

Trauma can play a hand when it comes to the development of ADHD; it is not yet exactly clear what the nature and extent of its impact is, making it somewhat complex. These distressing events are referred to as adverse childhood experiences (ACEs) and include traumatic events such as witnessing violence, experiencing direct abuse or neglect, and living in an unstable or unsafe environment. The likelihood of being diagnosed with ADHD is a lot higher in children with ACEs compared to children without ACEs (Brown et al., 2017). Additionally, people with ADHD are a lot more susceptible to experiencing further ACEs due to a "cycle of adversity" fueled by ADHD symptoms, which pose significant challenges in daily functioning (Lugo-Candelas et al., 2020).

Prenatal and Early Life Factors

Complications that affect fetal development during pregnancy and birth complications have also been potential culprits for ADHD. Let us have a look at these factors:

Pregnancy

The following factors and complications with fetal development could also be linked to ADHD:

- **Neurotoxins:** Exposure to chemicals, including some pesticides and lead, may be linked to ADHD (Yu et al., 2016).
- **Prenatal smoking:** It's no secret that smoking is incredibly detrimental to health, so it should not come as a surprise that, according to research, the chances of ADHD are 2.64 times higher when smoking during pregnancy (Han et al., 2015a). However, a 2022 study suggested that while an association may exist, it's unlikely to be casual (Haan et al., 2022).
- **Alcohol consumption:** Prenatal alcohol exposure will elevate the likelihood of ADHD in children by 1.55 times more (Han et al., 2015b).
- **Low birth weight:** Weight plays a significant role when it comes to the likelihood of having ADHD. A study conducted in 2018 found that babies who weighed under 3.3 lb were twice as likely to have ADHD, and babies under 2.2 lb faced a significant fourfold increase in likelihood (Rapaport, 2017).

INTERACTIVE ELEMENT

Who holds the grand record for the most decorated Olympian ever? None other than Mister Michael Phelps! What a legend! Michael faced various challenges during childhood, including ADHD, struggling to maintain focus, and bullying as well, making his path anything but smooth.

Despite skepticism surrounding his abilities and initial dislike for swimming, Michael found unexpected solace in the water, making him feel that this was one place where he had control. As fast as he cut through the water, it slowed down his brain, becoming his transformative outlet. Not being able to sit through class, Michael was diagnosed with ADHD in sixth grade, but that never dampened his desire to excel, and he became a nationally-ranked swimmer by the early age of 10. Bob Bowman, an acclaimed coach, spotted Michael's exceptional talent and believed in his potential for greatness despite the challenges and their differences.

Isn't it ironic how a child who could not sit still during one class could swim for three hours after school? Michael defied all expectations, perhaps even his own, with his initial aversion to swimming. Beyond his multiple legendary Olympic feats, Michael advocates for healthy living and water safety for youth. Through his foundation, he aspires to provide a haven for children with ADHD, showcasing the limitless possibilities of transformation, strength, and passion. His story shows that overcoming challenges and achieving greatness against all odds is entirely possible.

It's okay to exhale now that it is understood that there is nothing you have done or could have done to cause your child to have ADHD; pack the lingering guilt in the bag. It's time to prioritize more proactive steps to manage this journey best. Let us forge ahead and hone in on the symptoms and how they can be confused with other conditions.

2

RECOGNIZING THE VAST SYMPTOMS OF ADHD

— DR. SEUSS

It's certainly not a state secret that parenting comes with challenges. Now, sprinkle ADHD into the mix, and you've got yourself the ultimate challenge package.

Let's be honest: raising a child diagnosed with ADHD is not for the fainthearted; at times, it feels like you're in the ring with a heavy-weight champion where those tolerance levels may hit rock bottom. It's okay; you're not a terrible person. You're just a parent navigating the all-familiar rollercoaster of emotions. Let's take loneliness, sometimes self-imposed, because you're too drained. Hey, why risk an episode and damage-control exercises in public, right? Let's not forget the raised eyebrows and "If you can't control your kid ..." comments. Oh, and playgroups or childcare swaps? You're pretty much nonexistent. Then there's the unsolicited advice because everyone knows better. For crying out loud, a lot of times, the simplest things end up being high-stakes operations.

And then comes the guilt: "Why do I have no more patience to give?" "Why am I feeling like this?" Breathe; you're not a villain. You're human, and you are raising a child with ADHD. And, remember, there is hope on the horizon.

Let's look at strategies to help you navigate your emotional ship to brighter shores.

PAUSE FOR PARENTS

Just like there are measures you can take to improve the quality of life for your child with ADHD, there are steps you can take to help regulate and maintain your own mental and emotional health as a parent. So what's the solution? To reach out and find support. After all, if it takes a village to raise a child, raising a child with ADHD takes a whole city, right? And a little help, support, and understanding will be useful!

So many parents are out there, just like you, fighting the good fight. Not only are there parents who can resonate, but there are also oodles of support groups. And, thanks to modern wonders, such as the internet, tapping into these resources for much-needed support is simply a click away! These groups, networks, and communities offer a safe place to spill the beans and share concerns, experiences, and advice—no judgmental brows or unsolicited pointers. And, trust me, there is some great advice out there, such as making your home more ADHD-friendly and loads of other tips, and most importantly, social support to combat those feelings of isolation.

Some genuinely great groups and organizations that are most certainly worthwhile looking into include:

- CHADD (Children and Adults with Attention Deficit Hyperactivity Disorder)
- CHADD's ADHD Parents Together
- Learning Disabilities Association of America
- ADDA (Attention Deficit Disorder Association)
- ADHD Parents Together
- ADDitude Magazine's forum
- ADHD&U Facebook Group

Another personal tip I would like to add is to stick to proper routines, approach life with an attitude of acceptance, and, most certainly not least, try to maintain your sense of humor.

AN OVERVIEW OF ADHD SYMPTOMS

Kids generally need help sitting still and paying attention, never mind waiting their turn. And let's not overlook acting impulsively.

However, for kids diagnosed with ADHD, these behaviors are even more amplified compared to their peers. As you can recall, in Chapter 1, we examined the distinctions between inattentiveness (difficulty concentrating and focusing) and hyperactivity and impulsiveness, focusing on the specific associated symptoms. This diagnosis, in turn, opens a whole other can of worms, bringing challenges to home life, school, and peer relationships.

One important thing to remember is that this has nothing to do with mischief or misunderstanding. Your child is facing a genuine struggle. Just like their diagnosis does not solely define a young warrior battling cancer, your child is also not solely defined by ADHD. And the same rings true when it comes to you as a parent. You're not an "ADHD parent." You're a parent navigating the battle with ADHD. With your understanding of ADHD symptoms, let's delve deeper into specific symptoms to expand your knowledge further.

Age-Specific Signs of ADHD

Spotting any ADHD signs in early childhood development would be like finding a needle in a haystack. Everything is explored, bounced, and climbed on, so how do you differentiate? All is not lost because there are some telltale signs that you can be wary of. And, better earlier than later when it comes to catching them, it's a game-changer!

Let's take a look at what you should be on the lookout for.

Signs in Toddlers and Preschoolers:

Let's kick off with the tiny tornadoes—toddlers and preschoolers. Spotting the signs could be tricky because they are naturally high-energy and somewhat unruly.

However, if these behaviors get too extreme, it might be time to pay closer attention. If they can't sit still, coupled with excessive talking, constant fidgeting, restless behaviors, and trouble concentrating, it will be best to consider a professional opinion.

I might add that some kids with ADHD can execute significant focus feats on things that interest them, such as video games or their favorite toys.

Signs in Elementary School Kids

Hyperactivity is not likely present in all children with ADHD. If it is, generally, it will be visible during the school-age years, along with other quirks and symptoms.

Focus? Planning? Decision-making? It's a real mission. Taking turns? Sharing? Letting others speak? It could be likened to an impossible mission. Then, we added homework and chores, which all became adventurous. They could also be on the accident-prone side of life. This is due to impulsivity. Keeping track of things? You might find more solace in a squirrel organizing a nut stash. Then, there might also be challenges when it comes to emotional regulation. When they're happy, you'll know about it. When they're frustrated, a bomb might explode.

Signs in Adolescents

During the teen years, hyperactivity slowly starts taking a back seat. However, restlessness and a couple of new culprits might still occur.

Time, organization, and motivation might all dive, and these, unfortunately, are very "costly" symptoms. Instant gratification and immediate rewards tend to become the aim of the game. Then, we also have the standard teen protocol—emotional drama. However, when it comes to a teen with ADHD, emotional regulation could be a severe concern, along with impulsivity. Risky adventures like alcohol, drugs, and, well, you know, the rest might come knocking. This all raises a big safety flag, especially if you factor in that they're hitting the road themselves during these years.

DOES GENDER PLAY A ROLE IN ADHD?

It's a different dance when it comes to the rate of diagnosis between boys and girls. It's almost like comparing apples to oranges because ADHD presents differently in each.

Regardless of these differences, there isn't a separate set of criteria for boys and girls. But every little detail counts when it comes to ADHD to be sure that it's not overlooked. All aspects should always be highlighted, irrespective of age and gender. In general, it's found that girls with ADHD are less disruptively flashy. This makes it a tad harder to spot, irrespective of whether they have similar symptoms to boys. Thus, girls might slip under the radar when it comes to diagnosis.

As of 2016, according to the Centers for Disease Control and Prevention (CDC), about 6.1 million kids in the United States had an ADHD diagnosis, and the rate of diagnosis is higher for boys, at 12.9%, compared to girls, at 5.6% (Jones, 2022). This is rather startling!

Let's break it down and look at boys and girls separately to get a clearer picture.

♀ *Girls*

When it comes to ADHD and girls, they tend to lean more toward the inattentive type of ADHD. But it's not a sealed deal because they may also still exhibit impulsive, inattentive, and hyperactive type ADHD. However, the inattentive type seems to be more prevalent.

Symptoms may include the following:

- anxiety
- low self-esteem
- inattentiveness
- lack of focus
- academic underachievement
- challenges with executive functioning
- lack of attention to detail
- careless errors
- trouble listening
- poor time management

- avoidance behavior when it comes to tasks that require sustained focus
- challenges with following through on tasks
- easily distracted
- forgetfulness
- misplacing things
- disorganization

Add to this the emotional aspect, and you will find that girls and women often internalize symptoms. This can manifest in various ways, such as somatic symptoms, lower self-esteem and self-image, and heightened emotional sensitivity.

♂ *Boys*

Ah, boys will be boys, as they say. And when it comes to ADHD, boys are more prone to displaying impulsive and hyperactive behaviors compared to girls. However, it's important not to rule out the presence of inattentive symptoms, as they may still be prevalent.

When it comes to boys, the following symptoms may be present:

- impulsivity
- overactive behavior
- aggressive behavior
- excessive talking
- constant fidgeting
- interrupting others
- difficulty remaining seated
- trouble waiting for their turns
- disruptive behavior
- inability to perform tasks quietly

In boys and men, externalizing behavior and having comorbid conditions are noted to be more prevalent. This could include things such as breaking rules, aggression, antisocial behavior, conduct disorder (CD), and oppositional defiant disorder (ODD).

You might have picked up that girls' symptoms seem more internal compared to those of boys, which are more external. It's almost as if boys take their symptoms out for a walk, making them easier to spot. But, it's still imperative to remember that when it comes to ADHD, it's not a one-size-fits-all scenario about spotting or exhibiting symptoms.

COEXISTING CONDITIONS AND OVERLAPPING SYMPTOMS

There is a very dark side to ADHD—it's not just a solo act and may occur with other coexisting conditions.

The stats are rather staggering! More than two-thirds of individuals with ADHD are juggling at least one other coexisting condition. What worsens matters is that a person may juggle multiple coexisting conditions. Unfortunately, this only adds to the existing challenges of navigating ADHD. Often, this may be overlooked because ADHD symptoms tend to grab the spotlight, overshadowing coexisting conditions. This adds a hidden layer of chaos that, when left unchecked, could spell severe disaster. Let's take a closer peek at which conditions are commonly exhibited alongside ADHD.

Mood Disorders

Mood disorders may be characterized by extreme mood fluctuations. Children grappling with mood disorders struggle to regulate their emotions and often experience crying spells, irritability, and gloomy moods. It's pivotal to never underestimate the impact of these disorders, as they are closely associated with conditions such as mania, bipolar disorder, and depression.

Sadly, 14% of children with ADHD have depression as a coexisting condition (CHADD, 2018b). Compare this to the 1% of children diagnosed solely with depression, and the disparity is genuinely heart-wrenching. In my personal experience, it was navigating through my son's depression that led us to the discovery of his ADHD, a crucial turning point in understanding his unique challenges and needs.

Learning Disorders

In the realm of learning disorders, a mere 5% of children without ADHD receive this diagnosis (CHADD, 2018b). Now, compare this to the whopping 50% of children with ADHD that have a coexisting learning disorder, and you will have a whole different landscape (CHADD, 2018b). Dyslexia and dyscalculia are the most prevalent learning disorders, including speech problems. This severely impedes the acquisition of new information, calculating, and reading proficiency for these kids.

Disruptive Behavior Disorders

Oppositional defiant disorder (ODD), which is characterized by trouble in rule adherence, assigning blame to others, lack of temper control, frequent arguing, bursts of anger, resentment, spite, and other vindictive behaviors, affects about 40% of people with ADHD.

Another disruptive behavior disorder, conduct disorder (CD), is present in 27% of children. This is generally exhibited through behaviors such as lying, stealing, skipping school, defiance of curfews, aggression toward people or animals, and destruction of property.

Anxiety

Anxiety causes excessive worry about an array of issues, causing a person to feel stressed, tense, and edgy, and is often coupled with disrupted sleep patterns. Regrettably, approximately 30% of children may receive a diagnosis of anxiety disorder in addition to their ADHD diagnosis.

Tics and Tourette Syndrome

Here's something to wrap your head around: Tics or Tourette syndrome is found in fewer than 10% of people diagnosed with ADHD. But, 60% to 80% of people with Tourette syndrome have ADHD! Say what? Tic is a condition where rapid, sudden vocalization or movements occur. Meanwhile, Tourette syndrome, on the other hand, is a more severe instance of tic disorder that involves added extras such as making weird noises along with other daily symptoms of tics. It is a much rarer condition than tics and is challenging to cope with.

Sleep Disorders

Struggles with both falling asleep and staying asleep pose a significant issue, as reported by anywhere from one-quarter to one-half of parents caring for children with ADHD. This is a devil of another kind, as it may be a symptom of ADHD, or it can exacerbate existing ADHD symptoms.

Substance Abuse

Young folks are already grappling with hormones. Add ADHD into the mix, and you have a greater susceptibility to early engagement in smoking, alcohol, and drug use. This is a grim aspect, given that it has been observed that youths with ADHD are twice as likely to have addictive tendencies compared to those without ADHD. However, it has been shown that when treated with stimulants, youths at this age are not more, even less, inclined toward stimulant abuse of sorts than others.

WHY A PROFESSIONAL DIAGNOSIS IS CRUCIAL

Understanding the nature of your challenges is crucial for employing the best possible strategies in any situation. And when it comes to ADHD, it's no different. In ADHD, a proper diagnosis is essential for effective treatment.

Having a proper diagnosis and effective treatment enhances the overall quality of life. It paves the way for targeted strategies that will deliver more positive changes compared to persisting with ineffective approaches.

Let's further hone in on the importance of a professional diagnosis.

- **Diagnostic criteria:** Having ADHD testing done by a qualified professional will swiftly pinpoint whether your child meets the ADHD criteria. These comprehensive tests evaluate a child's attention span, behavioral patterns, impulsivity, and hyperactivity. Proper ADHD testing provides you with more clarity. It unlocks a world of effective strategies, enabling you to provide adequate support.

- **Deeper understanding:** ADHD testing also dives deep into various aspects of a child's functioning, which include academic performance, social interactions, and emotional well-being. This highlights their strengths, weaknesses, and needs, providing valuable insights.
- **Better planning:** Testing will paint a clearer picture of an appropriate treatment plan. It's certainly not a one-size-fits-all situation and may require a combination of treatments. For instance, your child's treatment plan could be a mix of meds, behavioral therapy, and some educational tweaks.
- **Better self-awareness:** ADHD testing provides a child with a better understanding of their uniqueness. It's a golden ticket to self-awareness, which will empower them to better self-regulate, self-advocate, and develop a stash of coping strategies.
- **Better support:** ADHD testing generally involves a collaborative approach. Think of it as a team effort that gathers information from caregivers, parents, and teachers. This provides a comprehensive understanding of a child's behavior in different situations. And, for the grand finale, it sparks better communication, knowledge, and rock-solid support for a child among all parties involved.

INTERACTIVE ELEMENT

As parents, we have a rather hefty to-do list of responsibilities. And, right up there, we need to inspire our children. And this could be rather challenging when it comes to parenting a child with ADHD. Those attention spans? It can disappear in the blink of an eye! So, let's try something new here. Let's inspire them with a story that hits close to home, highlighting the bright side of ADHD, starring the dazzling Emma Watson.

Your "Earth residency" must be questioned if you aren't familiar with the infamous Harry Potter and his crew! Among these actors was Emma Watson, who portrayed Hermione Granger and bagged her global fame. But she's not just admired for her acting prowess; Emma has also publicly spilled the beans about her daily struggles with ADHD. Emma attributed her superpower—the ability to hyperfocus on activities and her passion for them—to ADHD. This allows her to fully immerse herself into any given character she portrays. Talk about turning lemons into lemonade! In 2015, she earned a prestigious spot on Time Magazine's 100 Most Influential People list! She is a living example that ADHD isn't a roadblock. Correctly understanding and managing the symptoms can unlock unique strengths and talents. Anyone with ADHD has superpowers they can tap into, such as hyperfocus. Do you need attention to detail? Perhaps some brilliant creative flair? Hyperfocus is the name of the game! This ability allowed various individuals with ADHD to reach heights others only dream of.

This story isn't just about Emma; it also amplifies the importance of neurodiversity. It's all about encouraging people to open up about their experiences living with ADHD and other neurological conditions, breaking down stigmas, and paving the way for a more inclusive society.

Now that you better understand the importance of a proper diagnosis, there is no denying that it's a critical stride in the right direction. I completely understand that a wave of overwhelm and anxiety might tag along amid your sense of relief. Remember, the best thing to do is to take it one step at a time. Thus, let's boost your confidence and familiarize yourself with the diagnosis process.

3

HOW THE DIAGNOSIS PROCESS WORKS

All the noise in my brain. I clamp it to the page so it will be still.

— BARBARA KINGSOLVER

Most of us have dabbled in journaling during childhood. The intriguing thing about this is how blissfully unaware we were of the potent force journaling holds. Oh yes, the power of putting pen to paper is undeniable when it comes to stress relief and mental health. Why?

Well, letting that ink flow and pouring out all those bottled-up thoughts and emotions allows you to liberate them from the recesses of your mind onto paper. This, in turn, enables you to observe them more objectively. We tend to accept our thoughts as full facts. But let me tell you, thoughts are most certainly not gospel truths, and accepting them as such is quite an anxiety-triggering task. Writing is an exploration beyond mere scribbles, which may help reduce symptoms of depression and anxiety, boost immunity, and improve memory.

So here's to the classic "dear diary," I say! Let's hone in and take a closer look at the profound artistry of journaling.

PAUSE FOR PARENTS

An essential thing about journaling is that it's your safe space to spill whatever's on your mind and find closure. And here's a great promise: There's no grammar police involved! Another essential thing to note when it comes to journaling is that it's a personal process.

This should not be a rigid process; keep it flexible to weave into your daily routine easily. Pair it with an activity that you already enjoy. That first-morning cuppa, for instance. Journaling is best avoided as part of your bedtime routine. The emotions that get inked onto paper may often be overwhelming and unpleasant. Thus, preventing intense dramas before you nod off is best.

Another critical element is to journal without judgment. It's not about grammar, context, or punctuation. As mentioned, it's a personal experience for your eyes and reflection alone. Now, you may journal in many ways, depending on your mood. You might have a vent session. In this case, structured journaling, where you keep a thought log that centers around the triggering event and replaces negativity with rational counterstatements, could be handy if you're feeling artsy, doodle, or create collages. You can also opt for storytelling or letter writing as alternatives. For beginners, prompts and guided journals are especially helpful if you are unsure where to start. Easy prompts such as "What am I grateful for?" and "What thoughts and mindsets hold me back in life?" are a couple of examples that will help get the ball rolling.

While we are still on the topic of prompts, let's look at a couple that will get that ink flowing and enhance your self-awareness. Be sure to expand on each of these questions and statements thoroughly:

- What inspires you the most?
- What five things about yourself would you like the world to know?
- What evokes warm feelings in your heart?
- List ten words that describe yourself.
- What will you do today to take better care of yourself?
- What is your favorite self-care practice?
- Describe your ideal day off.
- What makes you feel safe?
- What is the most challenging thing for you to do or accept?
- If you could bring about one improvement in your life, what would it be?

ADHD DIAGNOSTIC CRITERIA

Concluding if a child has ADHD is not a straightforward task, as you have noticed. Guidelines in the *American Psychiatric Association's Diagnostic and Statistical Manual Fifth Editon* (DSM-5) are utilized by healthcare providers to facilitate the diagnosis process. Indeed, it's quite a mouthful, but it's great to have such an invaluable resource, such as the DSM-5, ensuring proper diagnosis and treatment.

However, let's look at some of the criteria in condensed form for easier understanding. It's important to note that this does not authorize anyone to conclude their diagnosis. Only qualified healthcare practitioners can diagnose or treat ADHD. Thus, consider this a little inside scoop on the topic; every bit of information contributes to a better understanding!

DSM-5 Criteria for ADHD

In general, people with ADHD exhibit persistent patterns of inattention and hyperactivity-impulsivity that impede development and functioning. These two symptoms could either be exhibited separately or simultaneously.

Inattention: Let's start off with inattention symptoms. When it comes to children up to 16, at least six or more symptoms should be present; for adolescents, age 17 and older, and adults, a minimum of five symptoms must be present. These symptoms should be present for at least six months and inappropriate for the individual's developmental level (meaning they shouldn't match up with what's deemed "normal" for that age).

- Lack of close attention to detail and consistent careless mistakes in schoolwork, work, or other activities.
- Having difficulties in maintaining focus and attention on tasks and other activities.
- Following through on instructions and completing assignments, chores, or other responsibilities is challenging due to loss of focus/getting sidetracked.
- Challenges when it comes to the organization of tasks and activities.
- Having a solid reluctance when engaging in tasks requiring mental effort for sustained periods.
- Has a tendency to regularly lose/misplace items required for tasks and activities, such as pencils, books, tools, glasses, and other materials.
- Distraction is a common occurrence.

- Forgetfulness is a common occurrence in daily activities.

Hyperactivity and impulsivity: The criteria about age are the same as with inattention. Let's revise: When it comes to children up to 16, at least six or more symptoms should be present; for adolescents, age 17 and older, and adults, a minimum of five symptoms must be present. These symptoms should be present for at least six months and inappropriate for the individual's developmental level (meaning they shouldn't match up with what's deemed "normal" for that age).

- Constant fidgeting, tapping hands or feet, or restlessness, such as squirming in chairs.
- Unable to remain seated when required, often leading to leaving seats.
- Regularly running around and climbing about in inappropriate situations. Adolescents and adults may experience limited feelings of restlessness.
- Unable to participate in activities quietly.
- Constantly "on the go."
- Excessive talking.
- Blurting out of answers/responses before questions/sentences are completed.
- Struggle with waiting their turn.
- Often interrupting or intruding on others during games, conversations, and other activities.

Additionally, the following criteria must be met:

- Various inattentive or hyperactive-impulsive symptoms present before age 12.
- Various symptoms are present in at least two or more settings, such as home and school.

- It's evident that the symptoms impede the quality of social, school, or work functioning.
- The symptoms can't be attributed to any other mental health disorders, such as anxiety and mood disorders, personality disorders, and dissociative disorder. The symptoms also don't occur solely during schizophrenia or any other psychotic disorder.

Three different kinds of ADHD may occur based on the types of symptoms:

- **Combined presentation:** If enough symptoms of inattention and hyperactivity-impulsivity were present simultaneously for the past six months.
- **Predominantly inattentive presentation:** If enough symptoms of inattention, in the absence of hyperactivity-impulsivity symptoms, were present for the past six months.
- **Predominantly hyperactive-impulsive presentation:** If enough symptoms of hyperactivity-impulsivity, in the absence of inattention, were present for the past six months.

Remember that symptoms may change over time; thus, the presentation may also change.

WHO CAN DIAGNOSE ADHD?

Our diagnosis journey doesn't just end with the DSM-5. There are a couple more crucial facts to take into consideration. One key point is that even though ADHD is a common disorder, it is also often misunderstood, leading to high rates of misdiagnosis and undiagnosis.

Inaccuracies in diagnosis can significantly be detrimental to daily functioning, mental health, and fostering relationships, robbing individuals with ADHD of leading happy, fulfilled lives—something every single one of us has a right to. This emphasizes the importance of receiving a proper diagnosis and treatment from a qualified mental health professional. In general, most people diagnosed with ADHD rely on a combination of medication and psychological treatment. And, as you know, precision reigns king, given the critical nature of these aspects. First, familiarize yourself with the ADHD testing and diagnosis regulations in your country to be sure you're reaching out to the right experts. Trust me, some research will save you time, frustration, and money.

In most countries, an ADHD diagnosis made by a psychologist or neuropsychologist alone is not sufficient to access much-needed medications for treatment. Down under, in Australia, general practitioners can diagnose ADHD and prescribe certain medications without the involvement of a psychiatrist. However, a formal diagnosis from a psychiatrist is required for more comprehensive treatment, which is always necessary. In the U.S., both general practitioners and psychiatrists have the authority to confirm an ADHD diagnosis and initiate treatment. If you hop on over to Europe, countries like France, Germany, and the U.K. only allow for a diagnosis from a psychiatrist to access medications and support. General practitioners and psychologists can only then implement the recommended treatment.

Let's look at some pros and cons regarding various practitioners.

General Practitioners and Pediatricians

Family doctors, such as G.P.s or pediatricians, are the go-to options when addressing concerns related to ADHD. This is rightly so, as they can provide more clarity through conducting provisional testing, making use of questionnaires and scales, and, in some countries, even prescribing certain ADHD-related medications. They may also provide referrals to psychiatrists and psychologists for further treatment.

+ Pros

- Shorter wait times for appointments.
- Easily accessible.
- Access to certain medications without the need for formal consultations with a psychiatrist.

− Cons

- Non-medicated treatments such as behavioral therapy and counseling cannot be provided.
- The range of medications that can be prescribed for treatment is limited.

Neuropsychologists and Psychologists

When it comes to ADHD testing with a psychologist, you can anticipate a thorough assessment that will delve into childhood history, symptoms, and life circumstances, as well as diagnostic questionnaires and scale results.

When it comes to neuropsychologists, the same procedures may be followed. However, these specialists are trained to hone in on brain function and structure. They explore how abnormalities in these aspects impact cognition and behavior. So, it's safe to say that for a more specific insight into how neurological deficits in executive functioning may lead to an ADHD diagnosis, neuropsychologists are the specialists to turn to.

+ Pro

- Psychological treatment can be provided, such as ADHD coaching and cognitive behavioral therapy.

− Cons

- Consultation fees are generally costly.
- Medications cannot be prescribed.

Psychiatrists

These clinically trained specialists treat mental disorders and can provide a full diagnostic assessment for ADHD. This will also include an evaluation that will delve into childhood history, symptoms, life circumstances, diagnostic questionnaires, and scale results.

+ Pros

- The psychiatric assessments are thorough, considering various factors to form an accurate diagnosis.
- Can prescribe a variety of medications for treatment.

− Cons

- Consultation fees may be costly.
- Due to high demand, longer wait times may be expected.

Licensed Therapists and Counselors

As with psychiatrists, neuropsychologists, and psychologists, an ADHD diagnosis is provided by delving into childhood history, symptoms, and life circumstances, along with utilizing ADHD diagnostic questionnaires and scale results. However, therapists' and counselors' approaches incorporate counseling and therapy methods such as ADHD coaching and support groups. Thus, they tend to be more focused on addressing behavior in a caring and supportive manner.

+ Pro

- Psychological treatment in the form of cognitive behavioral therapy and ADHD coaching may be provided.

— Con

- No medication can be prescribed.

As you can see, various options are available when seeking a professional diagnosis. It's essential to weigh all the factors, such as time, cost, and recommended treatments. However, above all, the best fit is always the one that will improve the quality of life. Remember, there's no quick fix or magic shortcuts here; it's a journey.

WHAT TO EXPECT IN AN ADHD DIAGNOSIS ASSESSMENT

Let's talk "real-time" here regarding what you can expect with an ADHD diagnosis assessment. We are going to take a close-up look at the initial screening evaluation as well as the comprehensive evaluation. Consider that the diagnosis process may take different "routes" depending on where you find yourself.

Initial Screening Evaluation

Here's a quick tip before we delve into details: An excellent place to start would be to consult with your general practitioner and then take it from there—one step at a time.

- The first stop is an initial interview that will help determine if social, behavioral, emotional, academic, or work challenges might be attributed to or amplified by ADHD.
- The DSM-5 criteria will be used to assist in assessing whether the number and type of symptoms displayed could suggest the presence of ADHD. Suppose the criteria do point to the potential presence of ADHD. In that case, the next step will be to undergo a comprehensive evaluation.

Comprehensive Evaluation

The first step in a comprehensive evaluation involves a series of in-depth interviews with individuals familiar with your child to gather comprehensive background insights. This generally includes parents and caregivers.

- Next up is a core symptom history assessment, which may include a set of detailed questions as follows:
- What specific symptoms are present?
- When are these symptoms present?
- Are these symptoms consistent in various situations or in the same one?
- What is the onset age of these symptoms?
- Are these symptoms pervasive, and what's the typical duration?

- Are there factors that seem to alleviate these symptoms?
- To what extent do these symptoms impact your child's age-appropriate and daily routine functioning?

Then, a bio-psycho-social assessment is completed that includes historical aspects related to the following:

- Prenatal, early developmental history, and developmental milestones.
- Medical history, including hospitalizations, illnesses, and injuries.
- Family history, encompassing incidents of violence, separation, or any other forms of disruption/trauma.
- Current functioning, detailing a typical day in your child's life.
- Co-occurring concerns, such as depression, anxiety, anger regulation issues, and learning disabilities, to name a few.
- Academic and work history, highlighting their challenges and successes.
- Their unique abilities, strengths, and coping skills.
- Interaction with family and other social relationships.
- Any substance use is a consideration.
- An evaluation of mental status and temperament.
- Family history of ADHD or co-occurring disorders.
- Separate behavioral interviews or child play sessions are also conducted to discuss and observe concerning behaviors.
- ADHD behavior and self-report rating scales are administered.
- Individuals who regularly interact with your child, such as family members and other caregivers, may be asked to complete relevant rating scales.

- Observation of your child in their school and "natural" environments may be conducted.

Referrals for additional assessment may be made:

- To rule out any ADHD-like medical conditions, a screening, medical, neurodevelopmental, or pediatric, may be required.
- For any co-occurring disorders that may be present and to assess the needs and benefits of medication, a psychiatric evaluation may be conducted.
- For any possible learning disabilities, psychological testing may be done.
- Screening for vision, language, speech, and hearing may be conducted.

Subsequent appointments may be scheduled to:

- Review rating scales completed by parties involved in your child's daily life.
- Review of school records.
- Review of any pertinent medical records.
- Review of other assessment information.
- Summarize the assessment process, share findings, and discuss the diagnosis.
- Collaboration with parents, family, or caregivers to create a shared treatment plan.

The information avalanche might seem overwhelming at first, but remember, every step along the diagnosis journey is a step that will set your child up to live a whole, happy life. Let's look at how you can best prep for this process to help curb some of that initial overwhelm.

PREPARING FOR THE ASSESSMENT

Before your "debut" assessment appointment, you and your child must complete several online questionnaires. These will delve into general info about your child, including their developmental, behavioral, and medical history and family details. Then there's your "assessment toolkit," consisting of a handy set of things you should have ready to bring to your first evaluation.

Let's look at what your "assessment toolkit" should consist of.

Assessment Toolkit

- All your child's medical records.
- School report cards and other reports or information about your child's academic performance and behavior.
- Any additional testing results, such as achievement tests, personality assessments, I.Q. tests, and previous ADHD evaluations, along with the names and contact info of the individuals who conducted these tests.
- All the names and contact details of other adults and caregivers involved in your child's life, such as teachers and after-school care providers. They might also be requested to fill out forms.
- If applicable, bring along individualized education plans (IEPs).

Up next, prepare for a round of questions in the parent interview, some medical inquiries, and delving into some family matter info. Let's see what's coming your way.

Parent Interview

Firstly, having both parents present during the parent interview is optimal. You will be asked about the nitty-gritty of the ADHD or ADD symptoms and how they impact every corner of your child's life. Consider filling out checklists, rating scales, and forms for an extra information boost. From your side, prep for the interview by listing concerns about your child that you would like to address. Talking with teachers and other caregivers for more information and relevant observations is highly advisable.

Additionally, give the following questions a run-through to be sure you have the best possible answers to help facilitate a proper diagnosis:

- When did these concerns/symptoms initially arise?
- For how long have these concerns/symptoms persisted?
- In which settings and at which times are these concerns/symptoms prevalent—home, school, after-school activities, among peers, the neighborhood, or within your community?
- Do these concerns/symptoms exceed what is deemed normal or deviate from what is expected to be typical for other children of your child's age?

Medical Questions

Though it's a great start, you may need more than just reviewing medical records for your specialist. Thus, let's get you comfortable with some probing questions about your child's medical history. Some possible questions to prep for include:

- Do you have any family history of diagnosed behavioral issues, including ADHD or ADD?
- Were there any complications experienced during pregnancy?
- Has your child ever suffered from seizures or a head injury?
- If your child has been diagnosed with any chronic illness, how has it been managed?
- Has your child experienced any challenges with stool soiling or bedwetting?

Family Issues

Discussing family issues may not be a walk in the park. It could feel challenging or even irrelevant, but don't be afraid. Spill the beans and open up with your specialist because the more info they have, the better they can decipher what could influence your child's behavior. It's not just about the bad; mention your child's strengths to give a complete picture of who they are.

Let's look at some family-related questions that might come your way:

- Has your family experienced any recent significant changes, such as a new addition to the family, separation, relocation, or a school transition?
- Has your family experienced any chronic tension or discord?
- Is there anyone in your family grappling with issues such as health problems or addiction?
- Has your family experienced any significant losses, such as the death of a loved one or a pet?

INTERACTIVE ELEMENT

It's time for that all-important dose of inspiration and association! We are pulling some heavy support from actor Channing Tatum for this round.

Famous actor and model Channing makes no secret of the hurdles he confronted in school due to ADHD and dyslexia. Well, beyond being candid about his struggles, he has a powerful message. He beautifully emphasized the importance of the uniqueness of each person navigating these challenges and also strongly advocated for transforming these exact challenges into stepping stones for personal growth!

His personal experience with medications is marked by frustration as they didn't correctly address his learning needs. Yet, undeterred by these challenges, he embraced his uniqueness and went on to find solace in the arts, carving out a blockbuster film career and a newfound passion for sculpting.

And what exactly can we learn from this formidable actor? Embrace differences and embrace the uniqueness of your journey because embracing your individuality can unlock your passions and extraordinary success. Remember, your life and path are valuable, and your strengths and challenges can mold you into the remarkable individual you are.

Getting a proper diagnosis and finding the necessary support might be time-consuming. However, you can still have options for improving your child's behavior. Thus, let's forge forth and delve into some behavioral management strategies that will help alleviate challenges like meltdowns.

4

BEHAVIORAL MANAGEMENT STRATEGIES

 *When you own your breath, nobody can steal your peace.*

— UNKNOWN

Meltdowns and classic day-long silence threats are just a couple of familiar scenes, right? After all, who needs that ten-minute workout without the additional distraction of a vocal exercise or a peaceful nibble on some leftovers without a side of scolding? The frustration gets real at times, as does the advice.

I'm sure I can "hear" you resonate with an eye roll when someone drops the infamous unsolicited "Just breathe." I know you've tried to improve the crazy balancing act by incorporating a few more healthier habits. But, for some reason, time always plays hard to get. However, what if I told you that it's absolutely true? Just breathe! We can't live without love or oxygen, for that matter. Here's some food for thought—what if "Just breathe" is more than just a cliché? You know the body's primal "fight or flight" response. It's a great mechanism that makes us rise to the occasion in the face of challenges. Unfortunately, when this response is constantly provoked by mundane situations, it unleashes a slew of health issues. High blood pressure, suppressing the immune system, anxiety, stress, and depression are some of the unwelcome results.

Realistically, a stress-free life is nonexistent. So, we can't avoid stress, but we can choose how we respond to it. The relaxation response is our weapon—a state of rest that can be elicited in various ways. Mediation and yoga are some great examples, but I would like to hone in on something different: breathing techniques! Swapping out some carbon dioxide for fresh oxygen will work wonders to ease frustration and relieve unwanted stress.

PAUSE FOR PARENTS

If you find yourself amid a high-level stress or anxiety storm, breathe. Trust me, these techniques will induce a state of calm and relaxation. No fancy equipment is required; you can start with just five minutes daily. Hey, even two minutes will suffice for starters. Thus, you don't have to worry about it gobbling up too much of your precious time.

Though there is a prerequisite, you must do it several times throughout the day. Schedule it or breathe whenever needed, as long as you give it a whirl.

Deep Breathing

This technique will alleviate shortness of breath, release all the trapped air, and replace it with fresh oxygen, making you feel more centered and relaxed.

What to Do:

- You can do this either seated or standing.
- Slightly draw your elbows back and expand your chest.
- Inhale deeply through your nose.
- Hold your breath for five counts.
- Then, slowly exhale through your nose.

Resonant/Coherent Breathing

This breathing exercise requires you to breathe at a rate of five full breaths per minute. You can inhale and exhale for a count of five. This is excellent for reducing stress and increasing heart rate variability (HRV).

What to Do:

- You can do this either seated or standing.
- Inhale for a count of five.
- Then, exhale for a count of five.
- Repeat this pattern for at least five minutes.
- And there you go! Easy and simple, yet very powerful, and most certainly worth a try.

How Can Therapy Help?

Kids diagnosed with ADHD genuinely benefit from therapy, and one big reason for this is that it helps ease the difficult emotions coupled with this diagnosis. Therapy enables children to better cope with challenges, improving their confidence and aiding in the battle against feelings of anger, frustration, anxiety, and depression.

It's more than just a treatment; it's a valuable tool that improves their overall quality of life. Therapy empowers them to:

- be more organized,
- pay better attention,
- be more focused,
- improve their listening skills,
- socialize better, and
- experience fewer behavioral challenges.

How Does It Work and What Happens?

It's all about hands-on learning and a positive environment where your child feels supported and encouraged.

The therapist will interact by conjuring up ideas and activities covering aspects such as handling emotions, mastering attention, social skills, study skills, and even skills to better cope with anxiety. Parents are in on some sessions, too, which is excellent for learning handy tips and tricks to keep the lessons flowing at home. You will also talk with the therapist, answering a couple of questions to deepen their understanding of your child. But what exactly happens during these sessions?

- **Playing with a purpose:** Games that teach children how to follow directions, slow down, and give it another try without having a meltdown may be played. This is great for fostering self-control (such as waiting their turn), planning, organization, and how to pack things away.
- **Problem-solving:** Delving into ADHD-related problems experienced in different environments will be discussed. Finding solutions to these challenges is a collaborative effort involving the therapist, parents, and your child.

- **Talking and listening:** Children are taught to pay attention to their feelings and express them verbally instead of through actions. Discussing their feelings and actively listening helps children feel understood, improves attention, and enhances learning and listening skills.
- **Activities that teach lessons:** Lessons about emotions, understanding others, organization, and studying unfold through fun activities and worksheets.
- **Practicing new skills:** New skills such as breathing exercises and mindfulness may be taught to help enhance attention and calm body and mind.

How Can You Help?

Being diagnosed with ADHD is nobody's fault; thus, it is best to focus on turning challenges into opportunities and focus on learning during therapy sessions. You can take a few more steps to support improvement; let's delve into some details:

- **Friendly therapy:** It's all about your child; thus, ensuring they are comfortable with the therapist is pivotal. Do a bit of research and ask around. Check-in with your child's healthcare team and explore the CHADD website.
- **Consistency is key:** Never skip a session. Your child is learning; repetition is vital for those skills to become ingrained habits.
- **Teamwork is dreamwork:** Work with your child's therapist to find the best strategies and solutions for various behavioral challenges.
- **Practice makes perfect:** To reinforce the behaviors, ask your child's therapist what games, tips, and tricks you may incorporate at home to strengthen your child's learning.

- **Compassion is crucial:** Remember to approach every step with a solid dose of patience and warmth.

TYPES OF THERAPY FOR CHILDREN WITH ADHD

As each child and their ADHD journey is unique, we, as parents, are lucky to have ample options when it comes to therapy.

Just off the top of my head, there is behavioral therapy, cognitive behavioral therapy, play therapy, art therapy, and music therapy that have all proven invaluable. Without further ado, let's hone in on each for a better understanding of what's to be expected.

BEHAVIORAL THERAPY

Behavioral therapy shifts the focus onto actions, not emotions, helping your child turn disruptive negative energy into positive thoughts and actions. And this whole party starts with you as a parent.

- This form of therapy differs from psychotherapy, play therapy, ADHD coaching, or occupational therapy.
- ADHD coaches may be called in for some backup; remember, they aren't doctors or therapists.
- Behavioral therapy is as effective as medication in young children. Behavioral therapy is generally the only treatment used for children diagnosed with ADHD between the ages of four and five. However, in more severe cases, a doctor might prescribe medication.
- For children aged six years or older, behavioral therapy combined with medication (the multimodal approach) is generally recommended.

Now, what exactly is parent training?

Parent Training

Parents are the primary caregivers in behavioral therapy. Thus, you will require instruction and parent training to get the necessary know-how. Oh yes, it's all about your skills and approaches. Generally, you'll be well-polished after about eight sessions with a qualified therapist. Consider giving stress management an additional go. Let's have a quick rundown on the basics of getting started:

- You can choose an ADHD behavioral therapist or opt for some ADHD behavior therapy classes that empower parents to navigate the ADHD journey best.
- You will learn how to best respond to ADHD behaviors and establish rules and guidelines. This will instill positive behavior in your child and foster stronger bonds among everyone involved.
- Ask your general practitioner or find some classes and therapists under listings using terms like parent training, behavioral parent training, and behavioral management training for parents.

Simply put, pretty much anything with the words "parent," "training," and "behavior" will be worth looking into.

Behavioral Therapy and Children With ADHD

Through behavioral therapy, your child will be taught to muster up skills such as:

- Limiting disruptive behaviors
- Reinforcing positive behaviors,
- Expressing their emotions in a calm, more positive manner.

Some behavioral therapy techniques will include:

- **Token economy:** This is all about consequence and reward; just like a teacher gives stars for work well done, you can employ the same principles at home.
- **Positive reinforcement:** Use a reward system as encouragement for good behavior. If the work is done, they unlock an hour of playing video games, for instance.
- **Response cost:** This is the opposite of positive reinforcement, where a privilege is removed if unwanted behavior rears its head. No homework, no video games.
- **Time out:** We are all well familiar with this age-old tradition. Bad behavior is reprimanded by sitting quietly alone for a couple of minutes.

Remember that it's essential to set clear, reasonable goals and be consistent with rewards and consequences.

COGNITIVE BEHAVIORAL THERAPY

An increasingly favorable option for managing ADHD is cognitive behavioral therapy (CBT), which is used either in conjunction with medication or as an alternative. This form of therapy hones in on how thought influences emotions and behavior.

Let's get real for a moment about medication. There is no arguing that it's highly beneficial in some instances, offering rapid relief from symptoms. However, medication is only effective with continued use. On the flip side, we have therapy, which does take a little longer to work but offers long-term results. This makes therapy an excellent choice because the skills acquired, such as problem-solving, planning, decision-making, and organizational skills, will benefit your child throughout their lifetime.

CBT and Children With ADHD

CBT help your child identify thoughts that trigger negative emotions and actions and replace them with positive ones. It's great because these acquired skills and coping strategies enable your child to self-regulate and manage their feelings better. This is noteworthy considering that, as per a 2019 study (Sciberras et al., 2019), approximately 60% of children diagnosed with ADHD also grapple with anxiety.

The power of CBT lies in its capacity to reduce demoralizing thoughts and decrease anxiety. Negative thoughts such as hyper-focusing on mistakes over successes, blaming themselves for uncontrollable events, and feelings of inferiority, for example, are all significantly curbed. Let's consider a real-world scenario: Your child might think they are to blame because of another child's unwillingness to play. Through CBT therapy, your child learns to remind themselves that it might not be their fault and that there could be an undisclosed reason for the rejection unrelated to them.

Another significant aspect of CBT is that it makes task completion much easier by arming your child with the ability to break large tasks into smaller, more manageable ones. This is immensely helpful in curbing feelings of being overwhelmed.

PLAY THERAPY

Play therapy is an enjoyable and effective intervention method to eliminate any potential of an ADD or ADHD diagnosis, developmental delays, adjustment, or environmental concerns before a formal diagnosis.

It's about using therapeutic play as a preliminary step in the assessment and treatment process.

Play Therapy and Children With ADHD

However, play therapy isn't only reserved for pre-diagnosis scenarios; it's also an excellent supplementary treatment! It imparts crucial skills that help address emotional challenges that are commonly associated with ADD and ADHD. It helps them increase their sense of responsibility, improve emotional regulation, foster receptiveness when it comes to understanding and setting limits, boost self-esteem and confidence, and curb feelings of anxiety and depression.

ART THERAPY

Alternative therapies don't nearly get the attention they deserve. They are often overlooked as a method of treatment, considering their significant impact on addressing core challenges for children diagnosed with ADD and ADHD. Alternative therapies, such as play and art therapy, I feel deserve more attention.

Art therapy employs techniques involving nonverbal creative expression, which works wonders for channeling intense emotions and curbing emotional outbursts. This fantastical outlet quells those meltdowns and improves behavior, self-esteem, and confidence. And we all know that if life looks good in those areas, it flows over and positively affects all other aspects. The benefits have even been shown to increase attention span and focus!

Art Therapy and Children With ADHD

Given that art is a natural part of play in child development, art therapy abridges many challenges children with ADHD face at home and in the classroom, enabling them to explore their identity beyond societal labels.

Talking about labels, children with ADHD have to face a lot of challenges when it comes to labeling, generally emphasizing their negative behaviors. And naturally, it makes it hard for them to acknowledge or focus on their positives. This is precisely where art therapy reigns king; it helps children positively connect with their inner identity. This connection facilitates a smoother navigation through negative experiences.

Unfortunately, art therapy isn't commonly offered in schools or by therapists. Thus, expressing interest and seeking guidance from your therapist or educators about alternative therapies is highly suggested. It's important to note that art therapy does not replace traditional forms of treatment; however, it makes for a compelling supplemental resource.

MUSIC THERAPY

Another fantastic alternative therapy to consider is music therapy! It not only has a significant positive impact on brain function but also effectively reduces stress for individuals diagnosed with ADHD.

The intricate emotional, physical, and mental connections formed when we listen to music are the exact magical elements that tap into the complex relationships within the brain, helping address psychological and physical challenges. This form of psychotherapy, which includes a systematic intervention process, starts when the sweet sound of music enters your ears. Music therapy can involve various techniques, including listening, learning, and creating music. These techniques may include binaural beats, improvisation, songwriting, discussing musical experiences, or engaging in musical recreation. All these techniques yield significant positive results, and music creation is incredibly impactful.

Music Therapy and Children With ADHD

According to research, children with ADHD have experienced a significant improvement in symptoms when receiving music therapy or listening to background music (Jackson, 2003). Listening to and making some music helps with other challenges linked with ADHD, such as depression, adjustment disorders, and learning disorders.

Now, what else can music therapy do?

- Increase alertness
- Improve focus and self-confidence
- Enhance sleep
- Create a sense of calm
- Offer a safe and socially acceptable way to communicate and express oneself.
- Encourage creative problem-solving.

Depending on what the goal of treatment is, all genres of music have their significant benefits. Some good old rock music may aid motor functions, while relaxing music is preferable for calmness. But here is some rather exciting news: when it comes to music and children with ADHD, research has found that while actively engaging in music-making, children are symptom-free (Wilde & Welch, 2022). It is supposed that components of making music and creativity stimulate the mind in ways not affected by ADHD! Thus, this golden little fact could be leveraged through music therapy to help foster motivation in various aspects. It is essential to take note that ADHD cannot be cured, and none of these treatments will rid your child of their neurodivergence. However, they all significantly improve quality of life by better managing the challenges associated with ADHD. My son discovered a profound passion for music.

It helped him focus and was an excellent way to express himself. Despite his ADHD, he worked hard to earn a BSA degree in music. His success shows how powerful music can be in overcoming challenges.

One last helpful hint regarding therapy: many practical therapeutic techniques are offered online. Thus, you can tap into some valuable resources without leaving your home!

DEEP BREATHING FOR A LITTLE PERSON

Let's start at the very beginning and look at the rather intricate relationship between breath and the parasympathetic nervous system for a clearer understanding of the benefits of deep breathing.

We all have two significant "teams" inside our bodies: the parasympathetic nervous system (PSNS) and the sympathetic nervous system (SNS). These are two branches of our autonomic nervous system (ANS), which helps the body maintain a state of homeostasis, keeping everything nicely balanced. The PSNS is responsible for resting and digesting, and the SNS handles stress-inducing stimuli and the fight-or-flight response. Both affect your breathing, and when it comes to deep breathing, the PSNS takes center stage, activating a state of relaxation and calm.

Next up is the vagus nerve, a cranial nerve that's a special messenger carrying information from the brain to the body's organs. You can see it as the helper of the PSNS, returning the body to a balanced state after stress. The vagus nerve facilitates heart rate regulation, slowing down your heart rate when things go too fast, and travels through a muscle, the diaphragm, which facilitates breathing. Then, there is the vagal tone, which indicates the vagus nerve's activity. If the vagal tone is strong, your body can calm down much faster after a stress response than a weak vagal tone. And that's your quick biology lesson; however, we are still going.

For the critical part, engaging in deep or diaphragmatic breathing activates the vagus nerve and the PSNS. Your heart rate slows, blood pressure drops, and stress hormones like cortisol decrease, making way for feel-good hormones like endorphins that boost mood and relaxation. It's remarkable how a few deep breaths can help you step into a more peaceful state, right?

Breathing for Kids

One of the best ways to support your child is by teaching them how deep breathing works, enhancing their understanding of how their bodies work in intense emotions. Just as with us adults, it will relax the body, refocus the mind, lower the heart rate, and reduce anxiety and stress.

There are various breathing exercises for kids, such as balloon breathing and bubble breathing, to name a few. However, belly breathing, or diaphragmatic breathing, is a simple and effective start that can be done discreetly, anytime, anywhere. Let's examine how you can equip them with this powerful tool to calm themselves during stressful moments.

What to Do:

- Ask your child to sit and breathe normally. Please pay attention to how they are feeling.
- Now, let them place one hand on their belly, right above the belly button, and their other hand on their chest.
- Now, let them inhale deeply through their nose and fill their lungs with air right down into their belly.
- As their belly fills with air and expands, ask your child to pay attention to how their bottom hand rises.
- Then, ask your child to slowly exhale through their mouth and feel their bottom hand lower back down again.
- Encourage a slow, even inhale and exhale by asking your child to either make a noise upon the exhalation, pretend they are blowing out candles, or hold one hand over their mouth to feel the air.
- Repeat this a couple of times, and ask your child how they feel afterward.

Tips and Tricks:

- Shallow chest breathing is linked to anxious breathing. Thus, if your child's hand on their chest is the only one moving up and down, make them aware of it and suggest they try to take deeper breaths into their belly.
- Having them lie down on their back might be easier initially to induce a state of calm.
- You can use a different object, such as a book, instead of hands if desired.

- It's best to practice deep breathing when your child is calm.
- Use counting by encouraging them to inhale for three counts, pause briefly, and then exhale slowly for four counts.
- Adjust and adapt the exercise to best suit your child's needs as long as it induces a state of calm.

CALMING TECHNIQUES

Every child is unique; thus, what might work wonders for one might not for another. However, engaging in particular activities at specific times, such as short bursts of physical activity or taking regular breaks and moving around whenever focus wanes, might be beneficial.

Some experts relate ADHD to the executive functioning of the brain, and this entails being able to pause and think, planning and organization, behavioral awareness, and switching between tasks. Emotional regulation involves tapping into all these aspects:

- Pausing and thinking.
- Paying attention to how your body feels.
- Recalling strategies that work.
- Choosing the best option.
- Organizing thoughts.
- Taking action at the right time.

That's a lot to do and could be very challenging for a child with ADHD. That's why doing a physical task beforehand can be somewhat helpful to release some pent-up energy, anxiety, and feeling overwhelmed. It can promote a more relaxed state.

Now, let's look at some fun activities to help with this.

Younger Kids

Wheelbarrow

- Let your child start in a push-up position, hands on the floor and legs straddling you.
- For added support, hold their hips.
- Move around the floor as they use their hands to explore, picking up objects along the way; you may even create a miniature obstacle course.
- As their ability improves, you can transition your support to their knees, then ankles, and even attempt going up steps.

Squeezing Games

- A great resistive activity involves squeezing bottles. Fill an empty toothpaste tube with liquid. Alternatively, you may use yogurt and let your child squeeze out the contents. Alternatively, you can make use of a stress ball.
- Another option is to take a plastic bag, make a small hole, fill it with soft salt or playdough, and let your child squeeze little snakes.

Paper Scrunching

- This activity is also very effective as a warm-up for drawing or writing.
- Make use of a large piece of paper; you can use junk mail or an old newspaper.
- Ask your child to scrunch it with both hands.
- After that, ask them to use only one hand without pressing it against any other part of their body, like their belly.

- Then, set up a target with a bin for them to throw the scrunched paper at and see if they can hit it.

These are just a few examples to get the ball rolling; other games/activities that are worth researching and giving a go include

- salt dough
- clothes pegs
- nuts and bolts
- meditation
- yoga
- relaxation exercises such as progressive muscle relaxation
- create a cooling-off/safe space
- a soothing bath or shower
- exercise
- listening to music
- getting out into nature
- painting and drawing
- allowing them to talk

Older Kids

Playing with clothes, pegs, and salt dough may not make the cut for an older child. Thus, we must switch strategies for those teary-eyed, emotional moments and outbursts. The following micro-techniques are fantastic shortcuts to cool down and instill some calm:

Five Senses Mindfulness Exercise

Name the following:

- Five things you can see around you.
- Some sounds you can hear around you.
- Things you smell in your environment.
- The taste in your mouth.
- The physical sensations you are experiencing.

EFT Tapping

This method requires tapping across specific body points to reduce stress. It might be much easier than meditation if your child struggles to quiet their mind.

- Identify the negative challenge or emotion.
- Rate it on a scale from 0 to 10, with 10 being the worst.
- Create a setup phrase before tapping, such as "Even with this problem, I completely accept myself." This will affirm self-acceptance.
- Tap the side of your hand with a "karate chop" as the setup statement is repeated three times.
- Then, use two or three fingers to tap through each of the following points in ascending order, tapping each point seven times:

  - Top of the head
  - Eyebrow
  - Side of the eye
  - Under the eye
  - Under the nose
  - Chin
  - Collarbone

    ◦ Under the arm
    ◦ Wrists

- After tapping each point, reassess the issue, rating the intensity on a scale of 0 to 10.
- Compare the reassessment results with the first results.
- Repeat the entire process until the intensity results are reduced as desired.
- Conclude with a couple of deep breaths and a positive affirmation.

Laughter

Laughter is indeed the best medicine, even if you fake it! Encourage your child to find reasons to laugh. This could be through watching a couple of funny videos online or exchanging a couple of jokes with each other. Please encourage them to consciously delve into the lighter side of life, especially when things seem overwhelming.

Some other great options worth looking into include:

- Create a music playlist.
- Design a vision board.
- Walk barefoot on the grass.
- Write down three things to be grateful for.

These are just a few suggestions; as they say, "Google is your friend," so take some time to explore all your available options that will best suit your child's needs.

ENCOURAGING THE RIGHT BEHAVIOR

Raising a child with ADHD will require some creativity when it comes to discipline. Understanding and employing different strategies is another way to enhance your shield's chances of success.

Let's explore some instrumental discipline strategies for managing challenging behavior:

- **Praise effort:** Acknowledge positive actions by providing constructive praise to motivate them. Focus on specific behaviors, such as waiting their turn or following directions.
- **Positive attention:** Positive attention is pivotal for decreasing attention-seeking behavior, enhancing the effectiveness of consequences, and fostering greater self-confidence. Positive playtime is an excellent way to dedicate one-on-one time to curb challenging behaviors.
- **Adequate instructions:** Providing clear instructions and breaking tasks down into smaller, more manageable steps will make it easier for a child with ADHD to hone their full attention and facilitate instruction effectiveness. Focus on one task at a time and avoid chain commands for better compliance.
- **Ignoring minor misbehaviors:** Ignoring small mishaps such as interruptions, loud noises, and whining, for instance, will send a message that such actions will not lead to any desired outcomes. Instead, acknowledge their need and underlying intent instead of honing in on the negative behavior.
- **Timeout:** Timeout is a valuable tool for aiding in self-regulation. Instead of seeing it as something negative,

rename it as "quiet time" and teach your child that it's a quiet moment that should be used to cool down and self-soothe to curb frustration and overwhelm.

- **Natural consequences:** Instead of handing out punishments left and right, make some room for natural consequences. It will save you and your child a lot of frustration. Instead, pack away that uneaten lunch and let hunger be the teacher, for instance. Next mealtime, they will feel more motivated to finish up.
- **Reward system:** A token economy system is an excellent example of a reward approach to promoting positive behaviors! Packing away toys or finishing homework, for instance, can earn them tokens, which they could later exchange for a meaningful reward. But don't hesitate to experiment with different approaches and see what motivates your child best.
- **Collaborate with teachers:** In some instances, adjustments may be required regarding schoolwork, such as extra test time. Thus, working with educators to establish collaborative behavior management is essential to enhancing your child's academic success.
- **Use "when" and "then" statements:** If you are approached with one of those unavoidable negotiations to engage in a different activity before a task is completed, say, "Yes, when you finish your homework, then you can play games for an hour." Remember, it's essential with younger children that the rewarding activity follows after completing a chore.

Be sure that your child correctly understands the rules, and last but not least, the aim of the game is progress, not perfection.

INTERACTIVE ELEMENT

Raven the Science Maven, an American science communicator, molecular biologist, and STEM educator, successfully navigated gifted and special education programs.

Despite facing challenges associated with ADHD, Raven Baxter discovered and pursued her passion for science and communication. She emphasizes that the realm of scientific discovery serves as a vast and exciting playground for individuals with ADHD. She encourages young enthusiasts to explore articles, ask questions, and watch intriguing documentaries to channel their excitement into engaging educational content.

Her beautiful story is a beacon of light for all diagnosed with ADHD, urging them to explore their instincts and interests. Working on doctoral research and developing science shows for a major network, she remains a strong advocate for seeking help, aligning with personal passions, exploring curiosity, and giving science a good go due to its endless possibilities.

A collaborative effort to improve behavior and therapy is enough to help manage symptoms. Yes, in some instances, medication might be necessary. And this is what we will be exploring in the upcoming chapter to ensure you comprehensively understand your options.

UNLOCK THE POWER OF GENEROSITY

"Alone, we can do so little; together, we can do so much."

— HELEN KELLER

In the spirit of collective support and shared journeys, your experience with "Parenting ADHD Kids Simplified" could light the way for others. It's not just about sharing insights; it's about building a community that uplifts and empowers every member, especially those feeling lost or overwhelmed.

Would you extend a hand to a fellow parent in need, even if you'll never meet?

Imagine a parent, much like you once were, searching for answers, support, and understanding in the maze of ADHD parenting. Your journey, knowledge, and encouragement could be the beacon they need.

Our book, "Parenting ADHD Kids Simplified," was born from a mission to demystify ADHD parenting and foster family harmony. But our reach is only as far as your voices take us. Your reviews help us connect, educate, and inspire parents across the globe.

By sharing your review, you're not just recommending a book; you're extending hope and practical help to those in need. Here's how your review can make an impact:

- Support another parent in finding effective strategies for daily challenges.
- Offer a glimpse of understanding and empathy to someone feeling isolated.
- Encourage a family on the brink of giving up to persevere and find new solutions.
- Share a success story that might resonate with someone else's situation.

Leave Your Mark in Less Than a Minute

Leaving a review is quick but carries immense value. To contribute your review, follow these simple steps:

- Scan the QR code below or click the link to navigate directly to our review section.
- Share your thoughts, experiences, and how the book has influenced your parenting journey.

https://www.amazon.com/review/create-review/?ie=UTF8&
channel=glance-detail&asin=B0D11R27P1

If helping anonymously aligns with your spirit of generosity, then you are indeed a part of our tribe. Your review not only helps a parent in need but also joins us in the mission to make ADHD parenting a journey of growth, understanding, and joy.

Your support is invaluable, and together, we can create waves of positive change. Thank you for considering this gesture of kindness and for being a pivotal part of our community's strength.

With heartfelt gratitude, Lucy Marvar

P.S. - Remember, the wisdom you share does more than you know. If you believe this book can help another family navigate their ADHD journey, feel free to spread the word. Your recommendation is a powerful gift.

5

THE GREAT MEDICATION DEBATE

Taking care of yourself doesn't mean me first, it means me too.

— L.R. KNOST

How full is your cup? I'm not referring to your mug on the table; I'm addressing your physical and mental wellness.

Regarding these two aspects, "charity starts at home." This means that you have to prioritize filling your cup before you can pour it into the cups of others. After all, what would you pour from an empty cup in the first place? To effectively take care of others, you must take care of yourself first. Easier said than done, right? We have parental guilt, a tendency to overlook personal needs, and endless to-do lists! So, how do we fill our cups?

Regular self-care is needed to keep that cup filled to the brim. And no, it's not selfish; it's an expression of self-love. Regular self-care contributes to a sense of balance, enhancing your capacity to care for others. You must regularly check in with yourself, your emotions, and your energy levels to ensure your mental and physical well-being are in equilibrium. As you have noted, I use the word "regular" because it emphasizes the importance of making self-care a routine practice, not just an afterthought. This will ensure that your approach is proactive and not reactive, ensuring you have a vital buffer against feeling overwhelmed, anxious, and stressed. What does a typical "cup-check" or checking in with yourself look like?

It's simple, quick, and consists of key questions:

- How full is your cup?
- Do you need to pause and refill your cup?
- What will help you refill and restore your cup?
- What are the most effective methods to engage in regular self-care practices and cup-checks?

Let's delve into a couple of suggestions for inspiration.

PAUSE FOR PARENTS

It's not a groundbreaking fact that raising a child with any special needs is exhausting. But putting your well-being at the top of your to-do list is not a luxury; it's a necessity. You deserve good overall health and happiness, contributing to your excellence as a parent. Here are some lovely tailor-made self-care practices for parents raising a child with behavioral challenges:

Fuel Your Body

There is no shortage of cortisol, the stress hormone, in a parent raising a child with ADHD, and aiming to lower these cortisol levels is crucial. Regular physical activity, maintaining a healthy, balanced diet, taking multivitamins, and staying hydrated should be checked daily. You don't have to eat like a rabbit and become the next Olympic sprinter; adopt realistic and achievable habits to avoid unnecessary additional stress.

Respite Services

Another great weapon against those elevated cortisol levels is taking time out, stepping away from stressors, and relaxing. This simple practice significantly reduces harmful stress hormones; even dedicating five extra minutes in the morning will be a great starting point. A trusted friend or family member is a valuable option if more time is required. Alternatively, you can research and explore some local respite services for caregivers in your area.

Celebrate Yourself

Give yourself some credit, and it's most undoubtedly due because of all the hard work you consistently put in daily. Make a list of at least five accomplishments that you are proud of. Perhaps you reached a learning milestone with your child, or you know you gave your best efforts in all your tasks. It could be anything, great or small; it doesn't matter if you compliment, appreciate, and take some time to celebrate yourself. And don't be bashful about it; share it with your loved ones. This will foster trust and encourage everyone to focus on the positives, even amid challenges. The best part of it all? It doesn't cost a dime!

STIMULANTS VS. NON-STIMULANTS MEDICATIONS

ADHD treatment is multimodal, which involves various techniques and approaches simultaneously. We have already touched on the therapy topic, so let's delve into the realm of medication.

When it comes to ADHD medication, there are two categories: stimulant medication and non-stimulant medication. The type of medications used depends on factors such as treatment goals, medical history, potential side effects, and other medications being taken simultaneously. Both stimulant and non-stimulant medications enhance concentration and attentiveness while curbing impulsivity. Sounds promising, right? However, it's not a one-size-fits-all scenario; one category may outperform another individually. Their mechanisms of action, interactions with other medications, and side effect profiles are the key differentiations. Stimulant medications excel in effectiveness for symptom management by preventing the degradation and increasing the level of neurotransmitters such as dopamine, norepinephrine, and serotonin. Non-stimulant medications, though not all approved by the FDA; thus, they are used off-label, have also been shown to be effective in some patients with ADHD.

Stimulants

Stimulant medications are the first line of treatment for ADHD symptoms, except for children under six years of age, who are instead referred to behavioral therapists. These medications work through two main mechanisms: increasing the amount of neurotransmitters in the brain and alleviating hyperactivity and restlessness. All stimulants should be taken with utmost caution, and controlled dosages must be followed as prescribed.

Some stimulant medications include:

- Ritalin (methylphenidate) short-acting
- Concerta (methylphenidate hydrochloride ER) long-acting
- Adderall (amphetamine/dextroamphetamine) short-acting

- Adderall XR (amphetamine/dextroamphetamine) long-acting

The effects of stimulant medications vary; in general, you can expect them to work their magic very quickly, taking less than one hour with a duration of three to four hours. Due to the limited period of effectiveness, patients may require multiple dosages throughout the day.

You can expect two different forms: short-acting and long-acting.

Short-Acting

stimulant medications have a rapid onset, taking effect within one hour of administration, with effects lasting between three to four hours. They are generally used in the mornings for symptom control but avoided in the evenings, especially for schoolchildren.

Long-Acting

For patients who require multiple doses of medication or have trouble remembering to take their medicine, long-acting stimulant medications were developed to save the day. These medications also have a quick onset, taking effect in less than 1 hour but with a duration of up to 10 hours.

Non-Stimulants

When patients are unable to take or do not benefit from stimulant medications, non-stimulant medications, including antidepressants and previously used antihypertensive medications, are prescribed for ADHD. The non-stimulant medications work magic by increasing neurotransmitters in the brain and inhibiting their reuptake. As mentioned, it's not a one-size-fits-all scenario with medications. Although non-stimulant medicines work the same as stimulants, the difference lies in how effectively they curb the symptoms. The great news is that the FDA has approved three different non-stimulant medications for teenagers: guanfacine, atomoxetine, and clonidine. Non-stimulants, such as atomoxetine, should also be approached with caution. Patients taking antidepressants or anti-anxiety medications should best steer clear to avoid serotonin syndrome (serotonin syndrome is a severe drug reaction that is brought on by medicines that elevate levels of serotonin in the body, leading to extreme nerve cell activity and other dangerous symptoms). Additionally, combining non-stimulants with stimulants is also a "no-go" due to the heightened risk of serotonin syndrome.

Some non-stimulant medications include:

- Intuniv (Guanfacine)
- Strattera (Atomoxetine)
- Wellbutrin SR and Wellbutrin XL (Bupropion)

The effectiveness of non-stimulants varies depending on the specific medication. For example, it can take weeks with atomoxetine and up to one month with bupropion to take effect.

COMMONLY PRESCRIBED DRUGS FOR CHILDREN WITH ADHD

Considering ADHD medications for your child? Knowing what's what regarding risks, frequency, dosages, and how they work is best.

Adderall XR (amphetamine/dextroamphetamine)

In October 2022, a shortage was reported due in part to intermittent manufacturing delays.

- It can be used 1–3 times per day as a time-release stimulant: separate dose 4-6 hours apart
- Generally, it is the first treatment option for ADHD symptoms.
- Prescribed to children between the ages of 6 to 12.
- It has not been studied in children under the age of six.
- A federally controlled substance that carries a risk of dependence.
- Improvement of symptoms was observed in 70% to 80% of patients with ADHD (Advokat & Scheithauer, 2013).
- Used to improve focus.
- Used to reduce impulsivity.
- Used to reduce hyperactive behavior.
- Effect size (a statistical measure of treatment efficacy) is substantial.

Concerta (methylphenidate hydrochloride ER)

- Prescribed to children ages 6 and older, usually once a day.
- An extended-release delivery system central nervous system stimulant.
- Medication is periodically released due to its osmotically controlled release oral-delivery system (OROS).
- It contains methylphenidate, the same active ingredient in Ritalin, but it is twice the amount of Ritalin.
- Used as a long-term treatment.
- Used to reduce impulsivity.
- Used to increase focus and attention.

*Aptensio XR (**methylphenidate hydrochloride**) can be taken whole or can be opened to sprinkle in applesauce.*

*Daytrana (**methylphenidate**) is a transdermal patch.*

- Aptensio XR is used daily: used as a stimulant
- Daytrana patch is applied to the hip area two hours before an effect is needed, but no more than nine hours.
- Prescribed to children between the ages of 6 to 12.
- Off-label use in those under six.
- Not studied by the FDA in children under six years of age.
- Shown effective and safe for preschoolers down to age three.
- A federally controlled substance that carries a risk of dependence.
- Used to improve focus.
- Used to reduce impulsivity.
- Used to reduce hyperactive behavior.

The outer capsule of Aptensio dissolves, releasing 22% of the dosage, and three inner compartments release medication at different intervals. Employs a backloaded delivery system, producing increasing blood levels of methylphenidate over 10 hours, followed by a rapid decline. Available in branded and generic options with only one branded generic identical to Concerta. Avoid any substitutes for the authentic branded generic alternative as they are considered inferior; two generic alternatives have been FDA downgraded.

Dynavel XR (amphetamine sulfate)

- It can be used daily: 2.5mg up to 20mg increased in intervals of 2.5mg
- Extended released stimulant.
- Prescribed to children between the ages of 6 to 12 and adolescents.
- May be chewed or swallowed or prescribed as an oral suspension (liquid).
- Useful if your child does not like to swallow pills
- A federally controlled substance that carries a risk of dependence.
- Used to improve focus and attention
- Used to control behavior
- Used to improve listening skills and organization

Evekeo /Evekeo ODT (amphetamine sulfate)

- An immediate-release, short-acting oral disintegrating.
- Prescribed to children between the ages of 6 to 17 and adolescents.
- A federally controlled substance that carries a risk of dependence.
- Used to improve focus.
- Used to reduce impulsivity, distractibility and emotionality.
- Used to reduce hyperactive behavior.
- The long-term effects of amphetamine in children are not established.

Focalin and Focalin XR (Dexmethylphenidate hydrochloride)

- A once-daily central nervous system stimulant.
- Contains the same active ingredient as Ritalin and Daytrana.
- Prescribed to children between the ages of 6 to 12 and adolescents.
- It has not been studied in children under the age of six.
- A federally controlled substance that carries a risk of dependence.
- Used to improve focus and wakefulness
- Used to reduce impulsivity.
- Used to reduce hyperactive behavior.

Intuniv (Guanfacine hydrochloride)

- A once-daily, non-stimulant.
- Prescribed to children between the ages of 6 to 12 and adolescents.
- Off-label use for all ages.
- It has not been studied in children under the age of six.
- Not a controlled substance due to low risk of abuse or dependence.
- Used as monotherapy or to supplement stimulant medication.
- Effective for addressing ADHD symptoms not well-treated by stimulants.
- Used to better regulate emotional sensitivity, hyperarousal, social aggression, and rejection sensitivity.

Quillivant XR *(methylphenidate hydrochloride)*

- It is the only liquid, extended-release methylphenidate for ADHD.
- It contains the same active ingredient as Ritalin, Concerta, and Aptension.
- Prescribed to children between the ages of 6 to 12 and adolescents.
- It has not been studied in children under the age of six.
- A federally controlled substance that carries a risk of dependence.
- Used to improve focus.
- Used to reduce impulsivity.
- Used to reduce hyperactive behavior.

Ritalin *(methylphenidate hydrochloride)*

- Usually taken 1–3 times a day before meals, depending on whether it is immediate release or extended-release.
- A central nervous system stimulant
- The same active ingredient as Quillivant, Concerta, and Daytrana.
- FDA-approved for children between the ages of 6 to 12 and adolescents.
- A federally controlled substance that carries a risk of dependence.
- Used to improve focus.
- Used to reduce impulsivity.
- Used to reduce hyperactive behavior.

Strarrera (atomoxetine hydrochloride)

- Can be taken once a day or divided into two doses.
- Selective norepinephrine reuptake inhibitor (SNRI).
- A non-stimulant medication.
- Prescribed to children between the ages of 6 to 12 and adolescents.
- Not been studied in children under the age of six.
- Not considered a controlled substance by the Drug Enforcement Agency (DEA).
- Used to improve focus.
- Used to reduce impulsivity.
- It was FDA-approved in 2002 as the first non-stimulant medication for ADHD in the U.S.

Vyvanse (lisdexamfetamine dimesylate)

- A once-daily, timed-release stimulant medication.
- Prescribed to children between the ages of 6 to 12 and adolescents.
- Safety for children under the age of six has not been established.
- A federally controlled substance that carries a risk of dependence.
- It is considered an amphetamine, according to the FDA.
- Used to improve focus.
- Used to reduce impulsivity.
- Used to reduce hyperactive behavior.
- It is FDA-approved since 2007 as an ADHD treatment.

It's important to note that while these medications have similar goals, they don't work the same way for all children. Kids with ADHD may respond differently to different medications, so a healthcare provider might try several options to see which works best for an individual child.

In summary, ADHD medications, whether stimulants or non-stimulants, are designed to help manage symptoms by regulating certain neurotransmitters in the brain, but they may do so through different mechanisms and with varying degrees of effectiveness for each child.

WHAT ARE THE PROS AND CONS OF ADHD MEDICATION?

There's no arguing that the medication is a great help when it comes to treating children diagnosed with ADHD; however, it's essential to understand that it's not a magical cure. Thus, let's look at a survey conducted by Consumer Reports about the pros and cons of ADHD medication, highlighting the experiences of 934 parents (*Pros and Cons of ADHD Medication,* 2010).

Before we delve into the pros and cons, the survey revealed that a whopping 84% of families opted for medication and that more than half of the surveyed children had experimented with two or more medicines within the course of the past three years.

Please note that the subsequent findings are based on the Consumer Reports survey conducted in 2010 (*Pros and Cons of ADHD Medication,* 2010).

+ Pros

- ADHD medications have been proven to be effective in 60% to 80% of children and teenagers.
- Those prescribed these medications have experienced improved focus, impulse control, and reduced hyperactivity.

- An improvement in school behavior, home behavior, and academic performance has been noted.
- Rapid, positive changes were reported by parents whose children were prescribed amphetamines or methylphenidate.
- The medications facilitated improved symptom management, positively impacting daily functioning.

— Cons

- Unfortunately, no compelling evidence exists that ADHD medication benefits have a long-term efficacy beyond two years.
- Long-term consequences have also not yet been thoroughly evaluated.
- There are no conclusive comparative studies that determine which medications work best in specific circumstances.
- In rare cases, stimulant medicines have been associated with strokes, heart attacks, and even sudden death. Thus, children must be evaluated for any underlying heart issues before commencing with medication.
- Many children on medication might not even have ADHD or only present mild symptoms due to the possible subjective nature of an ADHD diagnosis.
- In reality, the most effective approach for treating ADHD consists of more than one approach (multimodal therapy), such as medication combined with behavior therapy.
- Though medication was considered helpful, 52% of parents said that they would have their children on medication again, whereas 44% would rather opt for alternative methods.

- Side effects, such as weight loss, irritability, decreased appetite, disrupted sleep, and elevated moods/energy, may be caused by amphetamines and methylphenidates despite their positive effects.
- Non-stimulant medications, such as Straterra, were perceived as less effective.
- Using stimulant-controlled substances may be a cause for concern and careful consideration.

Risks and Precautions

Yet again, navigating ADHD challenges is a unique journey for each. But, as you can see, even as helpful as medication is, it requires careful consideration. Knowledge is indeed power in this regard. Thus, let's hone in on the risks and precautions that should be taken.

It's pivotal that your healthcare provider is fully informed about any other prior or existing medical conditions, and stimulant medications or atomoxetine should be avoided at all costs if one of the following conditions is present:

- Heart failure
- Hypertension/high blood pressure
- Structural heart problems
- Heart rhythm problems

It's also important to inform your doctor if any of the following conditions have occurred or are present:

- Bipolar disorder
- Tourette syndrome between the ages of seven and nine.
- Hypertension

- Severe anorexia
- Florid psychosis
- Tachycardia
- Arrhythmias

Most importantly, "self-medicating" your child should undoubtedly be avoided. A professional should monitor dosages and interactions between other medications your child is taking. There is no straightforward right or wrong answer when it comes to medicine. Ultimately, the decision will rely on medical advice and what is best for the child.

ALTERNATIVE TREATMENTS FOR ADHD SYMPTOMS

Let's spread your wings and delve even more deeply, expanding your knowledge of ADHD treatment by looking at some other alternative treatment options.

Sleep

You are no stranger to the benefits of healthy, regular sleep, and I have some exciting news when it comes to your child with ADHD. Researchers at Murdoch Children's Research Institute and Deakin University conducted a study that revealed remarkable outcomes about the benefits of sleep for children with ADHD (Hiscock et al., 2015).

The study implemented a two-session program that improved children's sleep and ADHD symptoms, daily functioning, behavior, and overall quality of life! What's even better? These benefits lasted for at least 12 months! This places a significant emphasis on the potential long-term benefits of establishing a proper sleep routine in children with ADHD.

Tips and Tricks

- Establish and maintain a consistent bedtime routine.
- Avoid screen time or any disruptive activities before bedtime.
- Optimize the pre-bedtime routine with calming activities such as:

  - Reading
  - Quiet play
  - Massage
  - Dimmed lighting
  - White noise

- Engage in physical exercise, magic breathing, and patience stretching daily.
- Consume regular, healthy meals containing enough vegetables, high fiber, and protein.
- Ensure adequate amounts of sunlight.
- Steer clear of foods that contain artificial flavors and colorants, including sugary drinks, sweetened breakfast cereals, and undiluted juice.
- Sweet mint or chamomile tea are suitable options; however, be careful with caffeinated drinks, which have been used to reduce hyperactivity and impulsivity in children with ADHD.
- Address any sleep disruptors, such as snoring.
- Ask your healthcare provider about melatonin administration as a sleep enhancer.

Exercise

Here's some more great news! A recent study has confirmed the wonders of physical exercise for improving daily functioning in children with ADHD (Hillman et al., 2014).

This study took 221 children between the ages of seven and nine; some were required to participate in a physical activity program, and others were not. What were the findings? Well, it's rather significant! For starters, it showed that physical activity improved executive control in the brain, facilitating focus, working memory, and cognitive flexibility. Thus, getting busy and active is about having a healthy body and mind for your child, bringing about notable improvements in math and reading. Similar studies support these findings (Hoza et al., 2014). Thus, no more convincing is required here!

Tips and Tricks

Younger Kids

Adhering to a little workout that will release some of that pent-up energy may be challenging, especially for younger children. And let's not even mention those winter months where playing outside is very limited. But all is not lost. Shake things up a bit and engage in some online workouts that feature their favorite characters!

Here are a couple of suggestions that are well worth investigating:

- Mario Gym Class with Sweat Kids
- PopSugar Family Fitness Cardio
- Frozen Dance with Sam Cam's Dance Studio
- Minecraft Yoga with Cosmic Kids
- Indoor Workout: Exercise in the Jungle
- The Very Hungry Caterpillar with Cosmic Kids

Older Kids

Oh, what's there to say about the overactive, impulsive minds of teenagers? Now add those hormones and ADHD symptoms, and you have yourself something akin to the perfect storm. Yes, the perfect storm, because their immature judgment and desire for experimentation leave them even more susceptible to dangers, such as peer pressure, which could result in drug addiction and alcohol abuse.

This makes engaging in extracurricular activities so pivotal for them. Among an array of options, here are a couple to consider:

- Biking
- Swimming
- Martial arts
- Team sports
- Scouting
- Art
- Music
- Drama
- Storytelling
- Board games

Diet

Before we kick off with this section, it's important to note that the connection between diet and ADHD symptoms remains inconclusive. It's no new news that healthy food equals a healthy body and mind. However, no concrete evidence points to specific foods impacting ADHD symptoms.

Take the Western diet, for instance; we all know it's not exactly the healthiest out there due to being high in sugar and fat.

Additionally, higher ADHD rates have been linked to the Western diet. However, it has not been ruled as a cause of ADHD (Howard et al., 2010).

Let's consider food additives, often suggested to reduce symptoms: yet again, they lack robust evidence supporting their efficacy. Sugar is another example; yes, it does moderately intensify ADHD symptoms, but it doesn't cause ADHD (Jones et al., 1995). It's a delicate balancing act as supplements, such as vitamin B, omega-3, zinc, iron, and magnesium, pose their own risk when administered excessively but may be beneficial in alleviating ADHD symptoms in deficient children (Nigg & Holton, 2014). Talk about complicating matters: the effects of ADHD medication may suppress appetite, bringing along more challenges.

But what about herbs?

Unfortunately, there are not many studies that can vouch for the effectiveness of herbal treatments when it comes to ADHD. Some herbs, such as pine bark and Brahmi, have shown some promise but are inconclusive (Sarris et al., 2011). Let's explore six of the most popular herbs used in the context of ADHD.

Herbs

- **Ginkgo biloba:** Some folks claim they have experienced an improvement in ADHD symptoms. But, proceed with caution due to potential interactions with other medications.
- **Green oats:** Studies suggest that there is potential for improvement in attention and concentration (Berry et al., 2011).
- **Brahmi:** A study revealed that Brahmi positively affected symptoms in 85% of the children involved (Dave et al., 2014).

- **Ginseng:** A 2011 study on children found improved anxiety, personality, and social functioning (Lee et al., 2011). Another study conducted in 2020 with children found that when combined with omega-3, significant improvements in memory and attention occurred (Lee et al., 2020).
- **Pine bark extract:** A 2006 study in children showed reduced hyperactivity and improved concentration and focus (Trebatická et al., 2006). Other studies conducted in children using pine bark extract indicated normalization of antioxidant levels (Dvořáková et al., 2006). They reduced impulsivity and hyperactivity (Hsu et al., 2021).
- **Herbal teas:** Chamomile, lemongrass, and spearmint teas are deemed safe and generally used to improve sleep and promote relaxation.

Talk about options. Though it's great to have all this at your disposal, always consult your healthcare provider and other specialists for reputable advice and guidance. This is particularly important when considering herbal medications, as the FDA does not regulate these. None of these options should ever replace medical treatment.

INTERACTIVE ELEMENT

Scott Kelly was the first American to spend 340 days in space from Earth to space! And what's more? It's surprising, considering that Scott faced significant attention challenges as a child.

What made it even worse for Scott is the fact that he was born before ADHD was officially recognized, causing a whole lot of confusion and misunderstanding when it came to his inability to pay attention. During college, he stumbled upon Tom Wolfe's The

Right Stuff, which sparked his interest in becoming an astronaut. And, as they say, the rest was history! Despite his learning challenges, Scott went on to get an engineering degree, become a Navy pilot, and complete four space missions with NASA! Now retired, he is capturing his experiences in his memoir, *Endurance: My Year in Space and Our Journey to Mars.*

Scott is a living example of how challenges can be overcome through perseverance and the proper support, demonstrating that we all can discover our passions, irrespective of our diverse paths to success.

When it comes to children with ADHD, consistency is key and king! The next chapter will explore simple ways to initiate a more productive and enjoyable school life.

6

THRIVING IN SCHOOL

 *Anxiety does not empty tomorrow of its sorrows but only empties today of its strength.*

— CHARLES SPURGEON

The other day, I realized that parenting resembles living in a frat house. Sleep challenges, numerous breakages, a dash of politics—parenting is an extreme "sport!"

We can all associate with the chaos—those days where anxiety and depletion loom so loud that it's easier to spare your vocal cords and open a candy wrapper instead of calling for your kids to gain their attention. It's a lot to deal with; it can be overwhelming, and often, we feel compelled to push through. That might not always be the best cure; consider progressive muscle relaxation.

PMR is a beautiful technique that was pioneered in 1930 by Dr. Edmund Jacobson to help reduce anxiety. And we will undoubtedly be eternally grateful to Dr. Jacobson! This powerful technique involves alternating between relaxation and tension in major muscle groups. This helps you better distinguish between a tense or a relaxed muscle, putting you right in the driver's seat of your anxiety response.

Let's explore this valuable tool further and see how to hone it for your benefit.

PAUSE FOR PARENTS

Here's another step-by-step guide that you can add to your stress management toolbox that will improve your overall well-being in the long term. PMR is beneficial when it comes to relieving anxiety, stress, muscle tension, neck pain, migraines, lower back pain, and even high blood pressure.

What to Do:

- Find a quiet place without any distractions.
- You can either lie down or sit in a comfortable position.
- Place your hands on your lap or the arms of a chair.
- Breathe slowly and evenly throughout the entire exercise.
- Next, you will focus on specific areas of your body while keeping the rest relaxed.

Start with:

- **Forehead**: Squeeze your forehead muscles for 15 seconds, then slowly release the tension while counting for 30 seconds.
- **Jaw**: Again, squeeze your jaw muscles for 15 seconds, then slowly release the tension while counting for 30 seconds.
- **Neck and shoulders**: Raise your shoulders toward your ears, hold them for 15 seconds, then slowly release them while counting for 30 seconds.

- **Hands and arms**: Clench your hands into fists and pull them toward your chest, squeezing as tightly as possible. Hold it for 15 seconds, then slowly release it while counting for 30 seconds.
- **Buttocks**: Clench your buttocks to increase the tension over 15 seconds, then slowly release over 30 seconds.
- **Legs**: Increase the tension in your calves and quadriceps for 15 seconds, then slowly release over 30 seconds.
- **Feet**: Increase the tension in your feet and toes for 15 seconds, then slowly release over 30 seconds.

WHAT FORMS OF SUPPORT CAN SCHOOLS PROVIDE?

We can all do with a bit of extra support when it comes to parenting a child with ADHD and navigating school systems. And thank heavens that we do have options!

To meet the individual needs of children with ADHD, schools may accommodate behavioral classroom management, organizational training, special education services, or accommodations to help alleviate the impact of ADHD on their learning.

Have you ever heard of an Individualized Education Program (IEP)? It's a personalized plan established under the Individuals with Disabilities Education Act (IDEA) for eligible students in public and charter schools. However, regarding school support, remember that it will vary from country to country. Still, in most cases, IEP is standard. This specially developed plan facilitates students' individual strengths and challenges by incorporating special education instructions, services, and support systems. Evaluations will determine specific student needs to qualify for an IEP, ensuring the best support for their learning and developmental journey. What's great about having an IEP is its legal protection, which includes specific rights in school disciplinary matters and rights for parents to be actively involved in educational decisions.

Classroom management aims to foster positive behaviors through implementing reward systems, promoting constructive behavior, and using report cards. On the other hand, organizational training focuses on teaching skills such as planning, organization, time management, and reducing distractions to optimize learning. Then we have the "big guns," special education services and accommodations governed by laws such as the Individuals with Disabilities Education Act (IDEA) and Section 504 of the Rehabilitation Act of 1973. Individualized special education services are provided by IDEA. At the same time, Section 504 offers a 504 Plan, introducing alterations and services to the learning environment.

Now, what is the main difference between IEPs and 504 Plans? IEPs hone in on individualized special education services, and 504 plans bring about changes and services in a learning environment to ensure that a child's needs are met for optimal learning. Parents commonly find that more services are available through an IEP than a 504 Plan. Aside from this noteworthy aspect, there are similarities between IEPs and 504 plans in the accommodations they provide, which include the following:

- Tailored assignments
- Tailored instructions
- Additional test time
- Use of technology for tasks
- Additional breaks
- Assistance with organization
- Positive reinforcement
- Environmental changes to reduce distractions

Enhanced Parent-Teacher Communication

Of course, you love your child! And, of course, you will advocate for them to help them tackle life's challenges with better resilience!

Frustration arising from a lack of communication is always apparent among parents, teachers, and children grappling with ADHD. Despite teachers' best efforts, they may not always have comprehensive knowledge of how to support and motivate a child with ADHD effectively. This makes advocacy a vital tool to bridge numerous gaps, ensuring the best chances of success for children with ADHD in educational environments. Because children with ADHD generally showcase symptoms of impulsivity and inattention, putting their safety at risk, advocating for your child also ensures their physical safety.

Let's look at some key considerations to take into account to advocate for your child effectively.

Tips and Tricks

- Comprehend how your child's diagnosis impacts their education and identify improvement measures.
- Thoroughly familiarize yourself with your child's IEP. Don't hesitate to ask questions to gain clarity and address concerns.
- Participate actively in developing your child's IEP or 504 Plan.
- Understand your rights and your child's rights.
- Maintain open communication with your child's teachers.
- Always obtain written documentation, reports, and records from educators, administrators, and other professionals involved with your child.

- Plan in advance with teachers, establishing times that best suit all parties involved for meetings.
- Collaboratively establish realistic goals with your child and teachers to reach specific learning milestones.
- Listen attentively to feedback from educators. It might not always be easy, but it's all about being aware of the challenges and finding appropriate solutions.
- Share as much information about your child, including medical treatments, with educators for a comprehensive understanding of their challenges and encourage reciprocal sharing.
- Regularly check in with your child and ask them about their experiences in the classroom and on the playground.
- Always assume positive intent to foster mutual respect and understanding that will benefit your child.
- Remember that educators face their own challenges when working with lots of kids; frustration might creep in, something that even happens to us parents.
- Keep it cool, don't take things personally, and try not to point fingers and express anger. Instead, focus on being solution-driven.
- Always express gratitude and appreciation to educators for their efforts.
- Be sure teachers understand that supporting a pupil with ADHD is a work in progress. There are no quick fixes or cures.
- Ask for help and advice when needed. You are not alone on this journey; many have managed to navigate it successfully. So can you!

Time Management: A Life Skill for All

It's no enigma that planning and time management are some of the most notable challenges for children with ADHD, negatively impacting their productivity in various aspects. But don't forget, ADHD or not, they are still kids, and planning is not exactly a forte.

Interestingly enough, a 2019 review found that there might be a connection between the perception of time and ADHD. However, this is not subject to everyone with ADHD (Ptacek et al., 2019). So, what do time management issues mean in practical terms?

Individuals who struggle with time management may experience difficulty predicting task duration, promptly sequencing events, retrieving time-based information from working memory and estimating the passage of time. As parents, what can we do to help improve their time management skills?

You'll be surprised to see how straightforward and effective these strategies are if you adhere to them.

Daily To-Do Lists

Make a collaborative effort and create a daily to-do list where you and your child schedule mealtimes, chores, homework, and other activities. Be sure to discuss the estimated time for each task to streamline adherence to these routines. It's worth looking into using an ADHD Planner for Kids to boost organization and productivity.

Weekly Schedules

Similarly, create a schedule at the beginning of each week, covering all that is required of your child. A well-defined routine is a great way to curb feelings of overwhelm. Start from the top and block time for everything they need to do, from waking up to going to bed. And be sure to attend scheduling time for breaks.

Organize Workspaces

A cluttered workspace can make it hard for your child to maintain their focus. Thus, eliminate distractions and help them get some order with color-coded folders, organizers, and a couple of storage bins. Be sure to incorporate workspace organization as a scheduled maintenance task.

Attention Span Estimation

Underestimating how long tasks take to complete is a general thing for youngsters with ADHD. To-do lists and schedules are great. However, it would help if you had your child document the estimated and actual time for each task. This practice fosters a better understanding of time concepts. Step in and help out with keeping track. If discrepancies between estimation and duration are drastic, discuss them with your child, exploring possible reasons/distractions and solutions.

Time Restrictions

Kids are kids, and allocated time might not be used for intended purposes. You can combat this by setting start and end times for each task. You can add fun and make a game out of it, rewarding them if they complete the task before the timer runs out.

Help Them Better Understand Their ADHD

The better your child understands their ADHD symptoms, the better they can manage them. Ensure they have enough information, tools, and strategies to empower them to recognize their triggers and behaviors.

Time Management Apps

Self-control, timing, gaming, distractions! Oh, the list goes on. When it comes to youngsters with ADHD they require substantial assistance when it comes to time management. Leverage the wonders of modern technology and make use of some of the following apps for support:

- Todoist
- Happy Kids Timer
- RescueTime
- OFFTIME
- The Stopwatch Bomb Timer

The Pomodoro Technique

The Pomodoro technique is not any ordinary "sauce" of sorts; in fact, it's a highly effective strategy for people with ADHD. Consisting of a short burst of work followed by a break, the Pomodoro technique reduces overwhelm. It helps manage time spent on a task.

Generally, the technique consists of 25 minutes of work, followed by a 5-minute break; this equates to one Pomodoro. After seven Pomodoros, a more extended break is taken. Yet again, it's not a one-size-fits-all scenario. With ADHD children, trial and error will be involved based on their attention spans. This technique benefits individuals facing attention difficulties by breaking tasks into smaller, more manageable sections, making them much less daunting. Overwhelm and hyperfocus are curbed through the specified time limits, which significantly helps prevent burnout.

It's like finding that sweet spot between productivity and focus. Furthermore, studies have demonstrated that students who implement the Pomodoro technique exhibit improved time management skills (Kreider et al., 2019).

Tips and Tricks

Let's delve into some additional tips and tricks that will contribute to seamless family functioning.

- **Make it count:** Every minute squandered at work wastes time with your family. Buckle down and get work done, avoiding taking work home and encroaching on your valuable family time.
- **Plan ahead:** Plan your weeks in advance to ensure all requirements are scheduled and met. Put it up where everyone can see it and comprehend what's expected and happening.
- **Downtime:** Schedule some personal time to step out and relax. It's a form of self-care that will help you maintain a "full cup."
- **Communicate:** Allocate time for regular family gatherings, fostering communication through conversations or shared activities.
- **Delegate:** Give your children responsibilities to instill a sense of accountability. This will not only help lighten the load but also save a lot of energy spent on the reactive habit of instruction. It's not a magic cure, and guidance will always be necessary.
- **Buffer requests:** Ask them to clean up their room in ten minutes instead of immediately. Putting a time buffer into a request improves the chances of it getting done because you remove the immediacy.
- **Anchor points:** Whether it's a meal or doing a couple of chores together, establish some anchor points at least

once a week to help keep everyone grounded amid life's chaos.

- **Write things down:** Avoid only relying on memory. Free up some mental real estate and write things down for better follow-through, whether it be thoughts or tasks.
- **Outsource:** Time is valuable, and so is your energy. Consider outsourcing specific tasks, such as hiring extra help for home-related chores.
- **Meal planning:** Get everyone involved and create a weekly menu. This will save time on shopping, planning, prepping, cleaning, and keeping up with impromptu requests.
- **Limit screen time:** Limit screen time by using a timer and buffer warnings.
- **Time box:** Set time limits on all activities to help manage the less desirable tasks, such as chores, effectively.

Bonus Tips to Help Children With Schoolwork

Show me one child who truly enjoys homework—finding a pair of chicken teeth will be easier. However, for children with ADHD, homework may be extra torturous. What takes other kids a couple of minutes may consume a child with ADHD for a couple of hours!

Well, the good news is that homework doesn't have to ruin your child's day, or, for that matter, any parent's, because some great strategies will help get things done.

- **Create a homework station:** Set up a dedicated, distraction-free spot where homework can be done. Ideally, the seat should face a wall. Also, consider using a fan or playing white noise to drown out any additional distractions.

- **Split assignments:** Breaking up study time into smaller, mini assignments, as per the Pomodoro technique, for example, is a great way to improve focus and maintain motivation.
- **Stick to a schedule**: With time management being a challenge for kids with ADHD, a schedule is worth its weight in gold to bridge this problem and help them stay on track. Make use of a timer or apps to help set timeframes and deadlines.
- **Studying vs. medication:** ADHD medication may facilitate studying while still in effect. Thus, it's best to synchronize medication times with study sessions.
- **Motivate:** Always encourage your child by rewarding them for work well done.
- **Keep track:** Children are great at forgetting things, including handing in homework. Thus, implement a little folder system for new and completed assignments to better keep track of academic responsibilities.
- **Be proactive:** We all need a backup plan at times, and when it comes to ADHD, due dates, and schoolwork, things quickly get forgotten, lost, or misunderstood. Regularly get in touch and communicate with your child's teacher about upcoming assignments or expectations.
- **Find a tutor:** Nobody's perfect, and it's okay if you find it challenging to help with schoolwork. Find someone who can, such as a private tutor or high school student—as long as your child's needs are met.

Tips and Tricks

Here are some additional tips and tricks worth a go when navigating homework:

- **Be present:** Respect privacy, but make it known that you are there for support. Conduct regular check-ins to discuss progress and inquire if additional help is required.
- **Encourage movement:** Boost mental alertness by promoting physical activity. It could be anything from a quick walk to a bit of playtime.
- **Make it fun:** Spice things up by creating games around assignments by incorporating fun elements, such as reward systems triggered when tasks are completed within a set time.
- **Completion, not perfection:** Encourage completion, leaving the assessment of work quality to the teacher. You can always respond to teacher feedback for necessary adjustments.
- **Encourage problem-solving:** Yes, the frustration gets real, but instead of being impatient and doing the work for them, allow them to simmer over it. This will encourage them to explore through research and improve their problem-solving abilities.

INTERACTIVE ELEMENT

Aside from his significant accomplishments, such as pioneering the first synchronized sound cartoon, *Steamboat Willie,* and the ever-popular *Snow White and the Seven Dwarfs,* the legendary Walt Disney had a rather profound set of struggles to grapple with— dyslexia and ADHD.

Though these traits come with a whole list of challenges, Walt successfully tapped into some remarkable aspects of ADHD, such as sensitivity and creativity! Joining the Red Cross was one of his passions, aiding him in redirecting his focus and making multifaceted contributions to the world. And it doesn't end here; he confronted his learning disabilities and attended night classes for artists, honing his skills and leading him to great success. What an icon, known not only for his accomplishments but also for his compassionate nature, transcended his disabilities.

Using his challenges as stepping stones to forge his way into a prosperous life, Walt proved that ADHD, in truth, is not a setback. Instead, it's more akin to a magical toolbox filled with unique tools, ready to be unlocked and harnessed to accomplish extraordinary things.

All the aspects that we have covered thus far are going to have a positive impact on your family. However, some additional strategies to foster stronger relationships within the home remain, which we will cover in the subsequent chapter. Let's forge ahead!

7

HAPPINESS FOR THE WHOLE FAMILY

Wherever you are, be there totally.

— ECKHART TOLLE

If you're experiencing a slight bout of depression, chances are you are probably dwelling in the past. If you're feeling somewhat anxious, you're likely preoccupied with the future. Now, what does this all suggest? It's relatively straightforward—the best place to be is now.

The reality is that you can't change the past; you can only learn from it. And the only time you can do something about the future is in the present. Fretting about the future is certainly not a proactive step that will bring about significant changes, and neither is dwelling in the past. However, escaping these feelings of dread is often challenging, yet it's completely doable with a bit of mindfulness.

Mindfulness is a state of mind that is focused on the present moment. It's not shackled by past concerns or future speculation.

It's an awareness of thoughts, sensations, emotions, and actions without criticism or judgment. Mindfulness is magical for mental and emotional well-being, fostering a sense of emotional connection and focus and reducing stress and anxiety. Other benefits of regularly incorporating mindful practices into your daily routine include improved sleep and a decreased risk of chronic health issues.

Would you like to tap into this magical reservoir and give it a try?

PAUSE FOR PARENTS

Practicing mindfulness takes little time, and you don't have to be an expert yogi. You can engage in mindfulness anytime and anywhere. And when I say that, I mean it! On the train, the bus, at work, or first thing in the morning—just five minutes, that's all it takes.

Body Scan

How do you connect with your emotions from within? With a quick, straightforward body scan.

- Find a comfortable spot on the floor and lie down on your back with your palms facing up.
- Take a few deep breaths.
- Start mentally scanning your body, starting from your head and moving to your toes, or vice versa.
- Be sure to focus on one body part at a time.
- For every body part, ask yourself the following questions:

  - Do I feel sore or tense?
  - Am I experiencing any discomfort?

- ○ Has any previous discomfort subsided?
- ○ Does my body feel unusually hot or cold, considering the weather?
- ○ Once you have completed the entire body scan, slowly sit up and take a moment to reflect.
- ○ If any aspect grabs your attention during your experience, write it down for later reflection.

Sound of Silence

The inevitable chaos of everyday life can engulf us instantly, but simple silence is another secret weapon at your disposal. Silence is golden—a great mindfulness practice that fosters self-connection conserves energy, and improves memory.

- Find a quiet, distraction-free place where you won't be disturbed.
- Take a comfortable seated position.
- You may even find a visual focal point to concentrate on.
- Spend time with your thoughts without judging them; immerse yourself in the silence.
- After five minutes of silence, slowly get up and stretch lightly.

Pick a Color

The world is a canvas splashed with a spectrum of colors, each carrying significance and nostalgic sentiments for every individual. Some colors might make you happy, others excited; it's a tailor-made experience.

- Choose a color and name it.
- Think or say out loud how many things you can find that share this color. Yellow, for instance, would be bananas, lemons, etc.
- Next, reflect on how the color makes you feel.
- Do you like this color?
- Why or why not?
- Do you like the objects associated with this color?
- Why or why not?

EMOTIONAL INTELLIGENCE AND THE IMPACT ON ADHD

EI and EQ? No, it's not an acronym for new technology; it refers to emotional intelligence or emotional quotient. This is our capacity to perceive, interpret, demonstrate, control, evaluate, and express emotions for effective and constructive communication with others.

We all know how significant it is to master this ability. Effectively expressing and controlling our emotions is essential to navigating this world successfully. However, recognizing, interpreting, and responding to the feelings of others is equally important. EI consists of four different levels of emotional intelligence. Let's take a look at these four levels in order of complexity. Starting with the more advanced processes, which involve greater conscious involvement and regulating emotions, and ending with the basics, which include perceiving and expressing emotions.

- **Perceiving emotions:** To understand our feelings, firstly, we need to perceive them accurately, which also involves understanding nonverbal signals, including facial expressions and body language.

- **Reasoning with emotions:** We use emotions to trigger our thinking and cognitive activity in step two. Things that catch our attention elicit an emotional response, and this is due to our feelings that prioritize what we pay attention to and what we react to.
- **Understanding emotions:** We must always determine why someone feels a certain way because emotions have different reasons. For instance, if your coworker is angry, perhaps you were the trigger, or they have problems at home.
- **Managing emotions:** A big part of emotional intelligence lies in how you handle feelings, which entails effective control and reaction over your own and understanding those of others.

A lot is happening when it comes to emotional processing and EI. On top of that, one must also become aware of these internal processes. Oh, the complexities of emotions! This proves to be a lot harder for people with ADHD due to its adverse effects on executive functioning. This hampers awareness and emotional intelligence, particularly regarding being aware and regulating thoughts and actions.

How Is Your Emotional Intelligence?

Ah, the many battles we parents face. Last week, peanut butter and jelly was a hit, but this week, it's chocolate spread. Nobody told you; you only found out after serving the sandwich!

These battles can't be navigated purely on logic and reason. It would help if you had an added bit of magic in the form of awareness and empathy. Managing emotions and emotional awareness is an excellent place to start. If you can grasp these fundamentals well, you'll step into emotionally intelligent parenting! This is pure gold, as it fosters healthy emotional development in children.

What Do Emotionally Intelligent Parents Exactly Do?

- **Self-care:** Emotionally intelligent people understand that self-care is not selfish and prioritize it. They invest in their own needs, fostering a greater sense of patience and overall well-being.
- **Intrinsic motivation:** They help their children find reasons within as motivation, encouraging concepts such as choosing effort over outcome, goal setting, and embracing challenges.
- **Focus on connection:** They recognize the importance of being fully present and creating meaningful moments to foster solid parent-child bonds.
- **Practice emotion coaching:** They always engage in emotion coaching, acknowledging and validating their child's needs and feelings and instructing them on effective emotional regulation.
- **Acknowledge anxiety and fears:** Active listening is a pivotal part of the emotional intelligence parenting package. Along with a good dose of empathy, they recognize their children's emotions and equip them with practical coping tools to manage these emotions best.
- **Teach, not punish:** Discipline takes a new approach, prioritizing teaching over punishment. This helps establish consistent, respectful boundaries to keep those behaviors intact.
- **Instill values:** Emotionally intelligent parents lead by example, instilling their values in their children through discussion, reinforcement, and encouragement.

- **Manage screen time:** Exposure to screen time is regulated, limiting exposure to negativity in any form that could significantly impact behavior and mood.
- **Collaboration:** Collaboration is on the priority list to facilitate accountability and motivation. Engaging in team efforts for individual and collective goal setting, such as SMART goals, is a routine practice that ensures continuous growth.

Emotional Intelligence Tips and Tricks for the Whole Family:

To be socially intelligent, you must be emotionally intelligent. These abilities are as crucial as practical life skills and a solid education. And this holds for everyone, ADHD or not, including us adults.

Let's look at some pointers to brush up on emotional intelligence for the entire family, aiming to understand our emotions and those of others better.

- **Emotion vocabulary:** Make it a priority to understand and label emotions by articulating what is felt or experienced in words. Initiate sentences starting with "I am feeling angry/hurt/happy because …"
- **Accept emotions:** Recognize and accept what you or others are feeling. Validating emotions, even when unpleasant, is essential. It's okay to acknowledge and accept them.
- **Build recognition:** Foster emotional understanding and empathy by analyzing characters' emotions in stories (watching or reading), discussing their feelings, and relating to their experiences.

- **Reflect:** Reflect on emotions, asking yourself or your child how and why specific emotions are experienced. The big word when reflecting upon emotions is "why." For a child, it might be challenging to find the answer. Still, you can help them by posing additional questions and exploring potential solutions together.
- **Observe patterns:** Are there some problematic emotions that keep popping up? Look for any recurring patterns and dissect situations to unearth possible triggers. Recognizing triggers is a crucial step in improving emotional regulation.
- **Prepare:** If certain situations elicit negative emotions, prepare beforehand by using visualization. Try to see possible alternatives that could facilitate better outcomes. Or, if an event triggers anxiety, create a list of prompts to provide a structured approach for when things become overwhelming.
- **Break it down:** Break it down into more straightforward steps to curb feeling overwhelmed, whether a task or situation.
- **Be clear:** Clear expectations, clear communication, and consistent routines eliminate a lot of unclarity, consequently minimizing negative emotions.
- **Be in control:** Remember, no emotion is more significant than you, even if, at times, it may not feel that way. You are in control. You can always engage in mindfulness and relaxation practices to help curb negative emotions and regain control.
- **Understand what works:** Develop an awareness of soothing methods to help you feel centered and grounded. Thus, do a bit of reflection to establish a "calm go-to list" of things to do when the going gets tough.

- **Express:** Verbal communication may not always be the preferred method of emotional expression. Thus, engage in and teach different practices through which emotions can be expressed instead of suppressed, such as writing, drawing, dancing, or playing music.

HOW TO HANDLE SIBLING BEHAVIOR

There is no shortage of drama in any household, and conflict between kids is standard. As natural as this occurrence is, it's still unpleasant for siblings and parents.

Fairness, competition, inclusion, and avoidance are all part of the party, often accompanied by the added challenge of embarrassment for siblings without ADHD. But it's not just about the embarrassment; siblings without ADHD might also experience frustration, guilt, and "good kid" pressure. On the other hand, for a sibling with ADHD, feelings of jealousy toward their neurotypical siblings, resentment, and inadequacy may be experienced.

The million-dollar question is: How do we, as parents, juggle these complex dynamics?

We have to nurture resolution skills. Let's explore some strategies.

- **Emotional control:** Again, as a parent, you should lead by example and demonstrate emotional control, teaching your children how to respond to each other, regardless of ADHD appropriately. Teach them to approach situations compassionately and not lose sight of goals during heated moments.
- **Keep it fair:** Ensure all children feel heard and understood by establishing clear household rules. And don't forget to also implement a reward system for added motivation.

- **Quality over quantity:** Foster individual support and meet individual needs by spending one-on-one time with each child. The undivided attention will show care and forge a solid parent-child relationship.
- **Open communication:** Openly discuss challenges, including ADHD. Encourage discussions, share information, and always be available to answer questions.
- **Family routines:** Family routines should be established with specified roles for each child to boost self-esteem and share accountability.
- **Family activities:** Foster positive interaction and trust by arranging regular, fun, and enjoyable family nights. This will also urge siblings to step outside their typical habits.
- **Celebrate strengths:** Always highlight unique talents by celebrating each child's strengths and the importance of their individuality.
- **Enforce consequences:** Children should understand that every action has a reaction and there is a consequence for unacceptable behavior. Set clear rules around consequences for violations.
- **Take a break:** After a conflict, create a buffer period and separate siblings for 15 to 20 minutes, allowing the overwhelming emotions to settle. After the dust has settled, regroup and discuss what can be done to move forward in the best possible way.

COMMUNICATING WITH CALMNESS

For children with ADHD, language processing might sometimes pose a challenge, potentially taking longer to learn how to talk. Even if they are proficient at talking, ADHD symptoms make it hard for them to stay on topic, find the right words, and use correct grammar, causing them to overlook various conversational details.

The list of challenges continues beyond here. When it comes to communication, listening comprehension is impacted, which causes problems when handling noisy environments and rapidly spoken language. This, in turn, causes social complications, and they may experience difficulties engaging in situations with simultaneous activities. Then, the amount of information conveyed also needs to be clarified. Due to executive function impairments, children with ADHD may jumble information and are often wrongly labeled as having an auditory processing disorder, which means they have a problem with hearing, which is not the case.

Give the following strategies to bridge these challenges:

- **Recognize when your child is hearing and paying attention:** Eye contact is essential during communication. For children with ADHD, establishing eye contact during conversations is not a guarantee. Still, it doesn't mean that they're not listening. Some might fidget and seem distracted, making it essential always to understand and pay attention to their cues.
- **Keep it short and simple:** Kids are scattered little creatures, and giving them colossal tasks will not suffice. Break it up into shorter, more straightforward tasks with step-by-step instructions as they go along.
- **Communication strategies:** Get creative and employ some fun listening strategies. Introduce a "listening object," such as a ball or toy they can play with if you need them to listen. You can also use pictures to communicate what you require from them. For example, show a picture of a bubble bath for bath time.

- **Use visual aids:** An effective strategy for kids with ADHD is using visual aids. Create a poster of what is required with a sequence of pictures for activities like bathtime or bedtime. You can even create a visual timetable that outlines their schedule. Get them involved in the visual aid creation; it can be enjoyable and personalizing.
- **Give options:** If you give a child a choice, they are more likely to listen. It's a little hack that slows them down and involves them in decision-making. The magic lies in talking to them, not at them. Ask what they want to wear instead of stating it's time to get dressed.
- **Easy does it:** Stay calm and speak gently to avoid overstimulation. This is especially true when it comes to meltdowns. Step away and engage in a soothing activity that will pique their interest, such as building a tower.
- **Explain expectations:** You avoid unnecessary confusion and overwhelm when communicating expectations. This clarity further forges positive behavior.

ADHD AND CONFLICT RESOLUTION

Refusing to comply with rules and accepting punishment—well, that's pretty standard with kids. Now, with ADHD added into the mix, the volume of these challenges becomes more pronounced.

Troubles with executive functioning and emotional regulation are the big culprits. But all is not lost; as a parent, the secret lies in being responsive and not reactive. Pre-arranged interventions are great for reining in and redirecting unruly behaviors. Let's take a look at the Harmony Huddle.

- **Identify patterns:** Dedicate 15 minutes for a family discussion about meltdowns. Talk about triggers, characteristics, and signs. Dive into details such as contributing factors, counteractive measures, and ideal recovery times for each family member.

- **Your responses:** Reflect on your typical reaction to these situations. What can you do to help? What is the ideal way you could respond? Identify your strengths and areas for improvement to support your child's ADHD-related emotional regulation best.
- **Improve cooperation:** Undoubtedly, everyone prefers peace in a household over arguments and meltdowns. Ask every family member to share their opinions, including them in the planning and strategy process, gaining their interest and making them feel heard. This will nurture closeness, making everyone think they are part of a team.
- **Make a Harmony Huddle chart:** Keep the peace with a simple six-step structure. Follow the example outline below and create your own Harmony Huddle chart:

  - **Trigger:** If gaming is generally the root cause, implement definite time limits.
  - **Expected reactions:** Protesting, yelling, or arguing.
  - **Your general response:** Remove all screen time for the rest of the day.
  - **Your new response:** Implement the set time break before any escalation.
  - **Options**: Allow your child to choose between time apart for self-soothing or engaging in a calming activity together. Preferably, a set list of activities compiled beforehand would be great to choose from for time spent together.
  - **Recovery:** After the dust has settled, engage in a brief discussion about what happened, accountability, and possible solutions.

○ **Practice:** Remember, it's about progress, not perfection. Aim for realistic goals; it's a process that will require trial and error. And remember to practice patience and empathy.

INTERACTIVE ELEMENT

There's not much you can tell Justin Timberlake about what it feels like to struggle with ADD and OCD.

He openly shared his experiences in an interview, and it's the bag of tricks, including distractibility, forgetfulness, and a penchant for meticulously aligning objects. And, much like other remarkable individuals facing diverse disorders, he has not allowed these challenges to dim his light. Justin transformed these challenges into constructive outlets, such as his genuine love for live performances, which catapulted him to international pop stardom. This story will resonate with all those facing the struggles of ADHD and various other disorders, showing the importance of understanding and effectively managing these conditions.

Turn the negatives into positives by redirecting the energy into something more beneficial and aligned with yourself and your values; your possibilities are endless.

So, we have reached our final chapter. The concluding chapter will delve into prepping strategies to ensure children are ready for teenage year challenges and beyond!

8

NURTURING FUTURE SUCCESS

 *Let us be grateful to the people who make us happy; they are the charming gardeners who make our souls blossom.*

— MARCEL PROUST

L ife has ups and downs, but that's what makes life beautiful. It's effortless to celebrate and be grateful when things go as planned. But what about those dark days?

Well, the attitude of gratitude is like a GPS, navigating your heart to brighter places. However, we should not reserve the practice of gratitude just for gloomy days; it is a daily ritual. Being grateful will do more than get you extra sprinkles on your ice cream; it enhances sleep, boosts immunity, and uplifts your mood. It also significantly contributes to improving anxiety, depression, and pain and helps guard against diseases.

If there were a pill you could take daily to ward off all these issues, you would take it without thinking twice. Why not adopt a daily gratitude practice without hesitation? It's simple and accessible, and you can do it anytime, anywhere! It is not just wishful thinking; when you take time to be grateful, even for the small things, you release oxytocin, the happy hormone, also known as the love hormone. Is that just perfect? You can give yourself a good dose of love and spread it by expressing gratitude toward others.

Let's look at how you can step into the attitude of gratitude.

PAUSE FOR PARENTS

Oh, we humans naturally incline toward negativity. It's not anyone's fault; our wiring for survival causes this. We refer to this as negativity bias. In ancient times, focusing on potential threats was crucial for survival. However, it's time to shift our mindset in today's safer environment.

In the primitive days, being alert and focusing on predators were much more important than worrying about what was for dinner tonight. Naturally, this way of thinking overshadows the positives. You do not need to worry about a lion in your backyard; in today's safer environment, it's time to shift gears and change that mindset.

Various methods, such as meditation, journaling, or art, are used to practice gratitude and help reshape this bias. I want to introduce yet another simple process called the *gratitude jar*. This process involves daily notes of gratitude placed in a jar, providing a tangible record of joyful moments to reflect upon.

What to Do

You will need the following materials:

- a jar

- a pen
- paper
- optional decorative elements such as stickers, ribbons, or glitter
- write something you are grateful for daily, and pop the note into the jar.

You can do it as many times as you wish and write down as many things as you please daily.

Consider creating a gratitude jar for each family member; incorporating this practice into a family morning ritual can deepen the sense of gratitude.

WHY CHILDREN WITH ADHD NEED HOBBIES AND PASSIONS

Please take a moment and reflect on the remarkable and inspirational individuals we've delved into, all of whom encountered challenges like ADHD and ADD during their formative years. Despite being the disruptive figures in class, unable to sit still or grasp things quickly, look at where they all stand today. It's all because they delved into and discovered their passions, transcending the label of "the kid with ADHD" to become a source of inspiration.

Children with ADHD require an enjoyable outlet to manage hyperactivity and stress, highlighting the crucial role of hobbies. Amid their academic pressures, it's essential to communicate that academic success doesn't solely determine their worth or success. Instilling this principle nurtures a more open and balanced mindset. Hobbies not only offer a creative outlet for children with ADHD but also expose them to unconventional career paths.

Encouraging activities like playing musical instruments, engaging in arts, or participating in sports instills self-expression, skill development, and improved focus.

Another hurdle with ADHD, especially in teens, is that it can be particularly challenging to discover a singular passion due to difficulties in slowing down and engaging in quiet reflection. As a parent, you provide support, time, and opportunities for your children to explore and discover activities that bring them joy. Here are some strategies to assist children of all ages discover their unique passions: Guidance to Explore.

Encourage your teen to list potential interests and passions, including hobbies, activities, or objects that spark interest. Have them rank and rate each interest to prioritize and narrow things down.

External Support

Teens value parental input, even if one sometimes doesn't take the top spot on the list. It's a good idea to reach out and seek external input from other trusted individuals they hold in high regard. This approach will offer more insight and fresh perspectives.

PERSONALITY VS. PASSION

Talk about turning lemons into lemonade. Please pay close attention to challenging situations that regularly land them into hot soup; there might be a hidden clue to a passion there. If your teen talks excessively, they may have great leadership qualities, so pop them into group activities or leadership roles.

Passions Beyond Personal Enjoyment

At times, passions can stretch beyond oneself, extending past personal enjoyment. Explore activities that form part of a more significant cause, such as volunteer work or teamwork-oriented pursuits.

Evolution

Passion and talent are only sometimes an immediate fit; sometimes, they need time to evolve and align. Identify activities your teen loves to boost confidence in that ability and brush up on skills, fostering the transformation of passion into talent.

Maintain Focus

When a passion sets in and takes hold, it may easily overshadow other tasks and goals. To prevent this, encourage positive self-talk and accountability to keep them on track and engaged with things that might feel unrelated to their big goals.

YOUR CHILD'S INTELLIGENCE AND SKILLS ARE NOT FIXED

Let's start in the simplest terms to define a growth mindset: you believe your brain can learn new things and grow.

Our minds are not set in stone; we have the power to mold and shape them, continuously learning and growing as life unfolds. Some people believe that we are either born as a "brainiac" or not, forever stuck with the hand we've been dealt, but this couldn't be further from the truth. Holding such a fixed mindset limits the belief in learning new things. Just as our bodies require regular physical exercise and healthy nutrition, so does our brain. Our brain will grow and perform optimally by continually training and nourishing it. Teaching a growth mindset is akin to building Rome; it's something other than something that will happen in a day. It is a process that involves recognizing old negative thought patterns and replacing them with new, more positive ones—much the same premise as CBT. Focusing on the positives, praising kids for their efforts, incorporating incentives, and leading by example are great starting points. Instill a "can do" attitude within your child. With this perspective, challenges become opportunities, and obstacles become stepping stones. Much of it also concerns self-talk; in this context, the word "yet" steps in as a powerful force. Instead of saying, "I can't," rephrase and swap it out with a mighty "I might not be able to, yet."

To lay new neural pathways and encourage them to fire and wire into a growth mindset, you should try the following activities:

- **Individual conferences:** Host mini-conferences at home to collaboratively discuss improvement areas. You can even involve your child's teacher and encourage your child to have one-on-one meetings addressing challenges independently. Focus on one aspect at a time to help boost confidence and prevent feeling overwhelmed.
- **Comparison chart:** Make a chart where you differentiate between a growth mindset and a fixed mindset, jotting down statements and traits in the appropriate category to help visually represent strengths and weaknesses.
- **Interviews:** Have regular interviews in the household to spice things up or encourage your child to conduct them among friends at school. Talk about challenges that each faces and collectively explore strategic solutions. Have a couple of follow-up interviews to foster care, empathy, and accountability. It's like a talk show promoting care,

compassion, responsibility, problem-solving, and social skills.

- **The hard thing rule:** Let your child choose a challenging task or activity they would generally try to avoid. It could be anything from conquering shoe-tying to mastering multiplications. Let them dive right in and practice it consistently to teach independence, perseverance, patience, and resilience.
- **Vocabulary instructions:** Write down and review growth mindset statements to integrate the terms into everyday vocabulary. The statements will provide greater insight into the meaning of a growth mindset, enhance vocabulary, and promote language skills.
- **Movies:** Watch movies where characters triumph over challenges to inspire your children. Dissect all the character traits and strategies they employed to overcome the challenges they faced. Some great films include *Finding Nemo*, *Good Will Hunting*, and *Remember the Titans*.
- **Books:** Who doesn't love a good read? Hunt some growth mindset books for youngsters to encourage and inspire them to explore different strategies. Some good reads worth diving into include *I Can't Do That, YET*, *Mistakes Are How I Learn*, and *A World Without Failures*.

RESILIENCE FOR LIFETIME SUCCESS

New Year's resolutions is like déjà vu. And the reason for that is that we all make them each year, kicking off with a vengeance, stumble, and generally end up at the same starting point again.

It's no different when it comes to children and the hopes and dreams they have for themselves at the start of a new school year. And, as with us all, they may find themselves stuck in a loop of lost goals and fading hope. But what can we as parents do to help them achieve their dreams and not end up in a repetitive loop of "wishful resolutions?"

Structure and Routine

As much as children and teens kick against structure and routine, it's necessary. It's something that provides them with a sense of safety and security. Yes, bedtime, meal times, homework time, house rules, and morning routines seem annoying, but they're pivotal. It's not about being rigid; it's about consistency. These predictable structures provide a backbone, making navigating the modern world and all its demands much more manageable.

Acceptance, Forgiveness, and Love

Kids with ADHD face negativity daily, whether it's feedback or labeling, due to symptoms like forgetfulness and impulsivity. Their emotional tanks get depleted, and the positives are so easily overlooked. As a parent, you need to refill your little tanks with a good dose of acceptance, forgiveness, and unconditional love. Acceptance and forgiveness do not imply that parents should overlook unacceptable behaviors; they should understand their challenges, correct the behavior, and always acknowledge and praise their efforts.

Don't Personalize Behavior

Behaviors in children and teens with ADHD can be on the wild side at times. Biting, lying, or kicking are often impulsive reactions. A couple of hurtful things may also be uttered, not to mention the coupled embarrassment. Don't take it personally;

these behaviors are not intentional. Keep an open heart, resist anger, and understand it's the challenges at play.

Make Room for Failure

We all slip up; nobody, including your child, is perfect. Leave room for error. Be there to offer support and guidance and help them learn from their mistakes, lessening their chances of repeating them. ADHD makes failure more common, so patience and resisting the urge to micromanage are critical.

Make Connections

Please encourage your child to connect with others by nurturing a strong family network at home and building enough confidence to reach out and establish ties with others, thereby gaining social support, enhancing social skills, and fostering resilience.

Help Others

Helping others is not only a noble quest but also empowering. Ask your child for help with tasks around the home, get them involved in volunteer work, and encourage them to reach out to others in need.

Pause:

Teach your child to pause and step back during challenging situations that might trigger overwhelm and anxiety. They should recognize that it's okay to experience these emotions. More importantly, teach them to focus on what they can control and let go of what they can't. Instill the importance of pausing and assessing the situation. A great way to help curb the overwhelm is to ask them to think about what advice they would give to a friend or loved one facing similar concerns.

Teach Self-Care

You understand the importance of self-care to keep your cup full, and it's no different for children. Ensure they get enough sleep, proper food, fun, and exercise for a well-balanced life to help them better navigate stressful times.

Goals:

Teach your child how to set realistic, attainable goals to foster resilience. Please enable them to take on more substantial tasks and challenges by breaking them down into smaller, more attainable steps, effectively managing overwhelm, and allowing them to focus on one specific thing at a time.

Accept Change

Change is often scary for youngsters, but you must let your child understand that it is an inevitable, fundamental part of life. Change forces us to step outside of our comfort zones and grow. Yet again, teach them to focus on what they can control amid modifications to make them more comfortable.

Happy Child = Independent Teen = Thriving Adult

What exactly does it entail for a teenager to be independent? It's all about taking on more responsibility, calling the shots, making their own decisions, trying new things, and gaining a deeper understanding of who they are.

Independence for a teenager is the key that unlocks adulthood, and along this adventure, they will need a lot of support, understanding, respect, and guidance. Let's look at some food for thought to help foster independence in your teen.

- Teens aren't adults; they still require support and structure, but at the same time, you will also have to respect their developmental needs. It's a delicate balance between support, structure, and space. Thus, allow them to spread their wings and explore their independence, but always keep a close eye and monitor them to provide a tweak if needed.
- Make a collaborative effort to establish goals and a motivation plan for school, social life, and other activities.
- Foster organizational skills by encouraging them to work out their effective daily routines. Motivate them to stick to their schedules and complete tasks.
- To make them feel heard and valued, involve them in serious decisions, such as establishing family rules and explaining the consequences of breaking them.
- Praise and acknowledgment are essential to fostering confidence. Thus, always be ready with a compliment when it's due.
- Encourage them to foster healthy connections and engage in extracurricular social group activities to improve their social skills and establish a strong support network. Let them reach out to others with similar interests. Also, teach them to show interest in others through gestures such as remembering birthdays and maintaining regular contact.
- Teach them how to effectively handle intense emotions and social challenges, such as rejection. They could adopt self-soothing strategies, such as going for a brisk walk or

listening to music, to calm down instead of turning into a reactive storm.

- Establish agreed-upon rules to proactively steer clear of conflicts as much as possible. Consistency is critical to avoiding confusion and meltdowns and upholding a structured and positive environment.
- Address concerns such as behaviors, curfews, and medication timing head-on. Direct communication will foster respect and mutual trust.
- There will inevitably be a lot of negotiating, which should be encouraged to improve problem-solving abilities, such as defining the problem, exploring possible solutions, choosing the best option, planning implementation, and renegotiating if required.
- They are teens and come with a buffet of bad decisions. So, you will have to lower the judgment calls and up your patience. The best thing you can do is to invest time in reflection, support, trust, and structure to keep the relationship healthy. Please give them the guidance they need to become responsible adults.

INTERACTIVE ELEMENT

One of the all-time greatest gymnasts, Simone Biles, has not only bagged seven gold Olympic medals and successfully navigated the sports world but has also gracefully stood up for her rights.

In these technological times, numerous dangers lurk with individuals who can instantly access any information with the click of a button, as was the exact case with Simone. In 2016, hackers violated her privacy by gaining access to her medical records and publicly disclosing her use of ADHD medication. She boldly stepped up to the plate, courageously acknowledged her ADHD diagnosis, and actively fought against the stigmas surrounding ADHD and its medications. She most eloquently put it forth: "Having ADHD and taking medicine for it is nothing to be ashamed of, nothing that I'm afraid to let people know."

She is a living example of overcoming challenges, standing up for your rights, and pursuing your dreams, regardless of stigmas or labels.

Having said this, let's now conclude our marvelous journey.

CONCLUSION

 *Everybody is a genius. But if you judge a fish by its ability to climb a tree, it will live its whole life believing that it is stupid.*

— ALBERT EINSTEIN

What a journey! There is much to be grateful for, much to learn, and so much purpose! Yes, it comes with challenges; however, what in life doesn't? There's always room for improvement, right? And yes, you might have a child or children that operate at total volume, but you have this. It's entirely doable.

As challenging as it may seem, even when life swallows you, remember that you matter because you have much to live for. Let's discuss the negativity bias. How about flipping the script? Instead of viewing it as a challenge, see it as a unique opportunity to elevate your child and yourself. ADHD necessitates a significant lifestyle adjustment; think of it as adopting a proper diet. It's not temporary or overnight; it's a lifestyle change. And might I add that most folks think the adjustment in place is solely for the benefit of a child with ADHD? No, it benefits everyone; it's a lifestyle upgrade. After all, isn't life about continuous learning and growth? You genuinely possess a golden ticket, even if it might not seem that way sometimes. Harsh words, right? However, consider it a front-row seat.

You are empowered to understand that "charity starts at home." To successfully navigate this ADHD journey, you must still respect yourself, prioritize self-care, and ensure your cup is full. Hence, it would help if you had a pause as a parent to be the best version of yourself for your family. Remember the saying, "Monkey see, monkey do?" Thus, don't hesitate to embrace your pause as a parent, or parents, and take care of yourselves. It's not selfish; these little "sponges" absorb and learn. Fostering positivity and love within yourself before you can radiate impactful love to others is one of the greatest lessons you can impart to your children.

Allow me to unabashedly say there is nothing wrong with putting yourself first as a parent. Most of us parents lack that due to guilt and endless to-do lists. Let your cup spill over; you will only function on a half-empty tank without that. And that's no good when it comes to the whole eclectic mix of children and problems. Oh no, you need to step up and step in. But do so with care and empathy toward yourself because your children will see and understand what is required for the foundations of their self-worth. And it might seem overwhelming, but trust me, you've got this, as so many before you serve as beacons of hope. ADHD is not a dead end; it's not a punishment. It needs a little bit of extra TLC. And, often, ADHD is not something that ticks societal boxes. However, if you can claw your way past the labels, past the stigma, ADHD, as you've seen, is instead an extraordinary ability, not a disability; it's akin to a superpower of sorts. These kids are wired differently. Channel that energy in the right direction; brace yourself to stand back because, aside from all the ADHD challenges, these kids have passion.

On our quest, we have dispelled some myths and unraveled some common misconceptions surrounding ADHD, allowing for a more holistic understanding of the matter. Armed with a greater insight into the true nature, causes, and prevalence of ADHD, you can now share the same wisdom with your child, teachers, and other caregivers for a deeper insight into their condition. Additionally, you are armed with a roadmap of the diagnosis process. It's important to remember that the diagnosis process is the very crucial first step toward understanding and support. Instead, it is an exciting endeavor to explore practical techniques and an array of diverse therapies, all of which could contribute to and help your child live a happy and fulfilled life that aligns with their needs. And trust me, simple techniques such as deep breathing are worth their weight in gold and should never be overlooked.

I encourage you to delve wholeheartedly into every technique and activity, including the "Pause for Parents." Everything stacks up, instilling greater confidence to navigate the complexities of ADHD with more resilience. Yes, the ADHD treatment landscape might come across as intricate at first. However, understanding your treatment options before stepping into this world, such as stimulants, non-stimulant medications, and a range of behavioral interventions, will empower you to make informed decisions for your child sooner rather than later.

Remember, there's no one-size-fits-all solution, and all the pros and cons deserve a thoughtful examination. It's not just about treatment and medication; it's also about the impact of their environments. Seeking out tailored strategies for their unique needs forms part of this package. Education and the school environment are integral to any child's life. For a child with ADHD, receiving proper academic support is of utmost importance to create an environment where their needs are fully understood, and cooperation is promoted. Foster effective communication with educators and encourage your child to do the same, thereby helping decipher complexities and challenges that might arise.

Teamwork makes the dream work, and as much as your child has ADHD, it still affects those around them—most importantly, family. You have to shine the spotlight on emotional intelligence here. This genuinely transformative power move will benefit the entire household, ADHD or not. Be sure to reflect and have proper communication strategies, sibling relationship insights, and severe conflict resolution skills to run a harmonious "ship." It's about keeping the peace in the present and nurturing future success. However, all you have is the present, and there's no better time than the present to gear your youngster up for the teenage years and beyond.

Encourage your child to dive right in and explore different passions. Introduce them to various sports, art, or volunteer work options. The important thing is to get out there and get active. It's all about finding the perfect outlet and finding passions that will stick and perfectly align with them, channeling their pent-up energy in healthy ways. This is a great way to foster a growth mindset and resilience, laying a solid foundation for future success.

And please pay attention to the all-important attitude of gratitude, yet another powerful tool in your emotional resilience arsenal to impart. This is not just reserved for sunny days but needs to be adhered to even through the dark ones, setting the perfect stage to navigate life's unexpected curveballs best. It's pivotal to do so consistently with every aspect of instilling sound moral principles. Yes, consistency is the key that will help lay those new neural pathways and foster a more positive mindset.

Throughout this book, you have been introduced to stories of inspiration from space to the swimming pool. We looked into legends such as Scott Kelly, Walt Disney, and Justin Timberlake, proving that no corner in life is unattainable for any child who faces challenges with ADHD. Instead, it's quite the opposite: ADHD is not a disability; it's a marvelous ability! It merely requires an exceptional key to unlock its full potential.

After all, life is all about perspective now. There is no doubt that raising a child with ADHD is puzzling, but with the new insights you have gained, it's a journey worth embracing. You are molding and building a bright future for a unique individual with an extraordinary superpower; you are the guiding light that can lead them to that magical key, unlocking a fantastic world filled with possibilities and a fulfilled life.

I have said it before and will most certainly repeat it! It's a unique journey, and what works for one might not work for another. Strategies differ, as do results; thus, consider it a tailor-made experience. It's a path of discovery, and you should embrace every moment. Celebrate your wins, big or small, learn from the losses, lay your footsteps with care and understanding, and know that you're not alone. You're a great parent; your dedication and love are a testament to that. With these strengths, you are more than capable of shaping a bright future for your child.

I am privileged to have shared one of the first steps on this most important journey of discovery with you. Remember, you've got this, and we've got this together! And if you found the information inspiring and helpful, I'd be grateful if you could share your thoughts through a review. This will help spread the love and, most importantly, contribute to spreading knowledge and awareness.

KEEPING THE GAME ALIVE

Your Journey Can Light the Way

As you turn the final page of "Parenting ADHD Kids Simplified," you stand at the end of one journey and the beginning of another. Armed with strategies for behavior management, tools for academic success, and keys to family harmony, you're now equipped to face the challenges of ADHD parenting with newfound confidence and grace.

But the game doesn't end here.

Your insights, experiences, and victories have immense power. By sharing your journey, you can guide other parents who are still navigating the maze, searching for the same clarity and support that you've found.

Why Your Review is a Beacon of Hope:

- **Empowerment:** Your story can inspire courage in others to embrace their journey with positivity and resilience.
- **Guidance:** Your review can highlight the most helpful aspects of the book, directing others toward the strategies that work.
- **Community:** Sharing your experience fosters a sense of belonging, reminding other parents that they are not alone in their struggles or triumphs.

How to Share Your Light:

- **Reflect on Your Journey:** Think about where you started, the challenges you faced, and how the book helped you navigate the parenting landscape of ADHD.
- **Write Your Review:** Visit the book's review section by scanning the QR code or clicking the provided link. Share your thoughts, insights, and how the book impacted your family life.
- **Pass It On:** Your review is more than just words; it's a lifeline, an invitation to a community where every parent has the support they need to thrive.

https://www.amazon.com/review/create-review/?ie=UTF8&
channel=glance-detail&asin=B0D11R27P1

In "Parenting ADHD Kids Simplified," we've embarked on this journey together, and now, it's your turn to keep the game alive. Your review not only celebrates your progress but also extends a hand to those still finding their way.

Thank you for choosing to be a part of this journey, for every challenge faced, and every small victory celebrated. Your voice is the echo that keeps the game alive, turning individual journeys into a collective adventure of growth, understanding, and unconditional support.

With deepest gratitude, Lucy Marvar

P.S. - Remember, your journey's insights are invaluable. By sharing your review, you're not just recommending a book; you're opening a door to a world of support, understanding, and shared success for families just like yours.

REFERENCES

1. ADDitude Editors. (2006, November 30). "None of us were trained how to be good parents:" An ADHD guide to behavior therapy. ADDitude. https://www.additudemag.com/using-behavior-therapy-with-your-child/

2. Addrc, A. (2014, September 9). The effects of ADHD on communication. ADD Resource Center. https://www.addrc.org/effects-adhd-communication/

3. ADHDaptive. (2023, May 9). Emma Watson and ADHD. ADHDaptive. https://adhdaptive.org/adhdaptive-blog/f/emma-watson-and-adhd

4. The ADHD diagnostic process. (2023). CHADD. https://chadd.org/for-professionals/the-adhd-diagnostic-process/

5. Advokat, C., & Scheithauer, M. (2013). Attention-deficit hyperactivity disorder (ADHD) stimulant medications as cognitive enhancers. Frontiers in Neuroscience, 7(82). https://doi.org/10.3389/fnins.2013.00082

6. Akita, L. G. (n.d.) Lailah Gifty Akita quotes. Goodreads. https://www.goodreads.com/quotes/7010722-never-be-afraid-to-travel-on-a-new-path

7. American Academy of Pediatrics. (2018, October 22). 8 ADHD myths & misconceptions. Healthy Children. https://www.healthychildren.org/English/health-issues/conditions/adhd/Pages/Myths-and-Misconceptions.aspx

8. American Psychological Association. (2020, August 26). Resilience guide for parents and teachers. American Psychological Association. https://www.apa.org/topics/resilience/guide-parents-teachers

9. Anderson, D. (2023). What is the difference between ADD and ADHD? Child Mind Institute. https://childmind.org/article/what-is-the-difference-between-add-and-adhd/

10. Anthony, K. (2017). What is EFT tapping? 5-Step technique for anxiety relief.

Healthline. [https://www.healthline.com/health/eft-tapping#treatment] (https://www.healthline.com/health/eft-tapping#treatment)

Continuing the APA format references:

11. Attention deficit hyperactivity disorder (ADHD): supporting teenagers. (2023, January 24). Raising Children Network. https://raisingchildren.net.au/teens/development/adhd/managing-adhd-12-18-years#building-independence-for-teenagers-with-adhd-nav-title

12. Belsky, G. (2022). What is an IEP? Understood. https://www.understood.org/en/articles/what-is-an-iep

13. Bennett, R. T. (n.d.). Roy T Bennett quotes. Goodreads. https://www.goodreads.com/quotes/7953983-start-each-day-with-a-positive-thought-and-a-grateful

14. Berry, N. M., Robinson, M. J., Bryan, J., Buckley, J. D., Murphy, K. J., & Howe, P. R. C. (2011). Acute effects of an Avena sativa herb extract on responses to the Stroop color–word test. The Journal of Alternative and Complementary Medicine, 17(7), 635–637. https://doi.org/10.1089/acm.2010.0450

15. Berry, P. (2020, October 9). Help your ADHD teenager find his passion: positive parenting. ADDitude. https://www.additudemag.com/wheres-the-passion/

16. BetterHelp Editorial Team. (2019, June 12). Music therapy for children with ADHD. Betterhelp. https://www.betterhelp.com/advice/adhd/if-your-child-has-adhd-music-therapy-can-help/

17. Bitsko, R. H., Claussen, A. H., Lichstein, J., Black, L. I., Jones, S. E., Danielson, M. L., Hoenig, J. M., Davis Jack, S. P., Brody, D. J., Gyawali, S., Maenner, M. J., Warner, M., Holland, K. M., Perou, R., Crosby, A. E., Blumberg, S. J., Avenevoli, S., Kaminski, J. W., Ghandour, R. M., & Meyer, L. N. (2022). Mental health surveillance among children — the United States, 2013–2019. MMWR Supplements, 71(2), 1–42. https://doi.org/10.15585/mmwr.su7102a1

18. Breathing exercises for kids. (2020). Children's Health. https://www.childrens.com/health-wellness/breathing-exercises-for-kids

19. Brown, N. M., Brown, S. N., Briggs, R. D., Germán, M., Belamarich, P. F., & Oyeku, S. O. (2017). Associations between adverse childhood experiences and

ADHD diagnosis and severity. Academic Pediatrics, 17(4), 349–355. https://doi.org/10.1016/j.acap.2016.08.013

20. Build emotional intelligence in your child with learning disabilities and ADHD. (2021, September 14). ldexplained. https://www.ldexplained.org/social-inclusion/social-and-emotional-skills/build-emotional-intelligence/

21. Calming and regulating activities for ADHD. (2023). Gympanzees. https://www.gymanzees.org/our-services/online-resource-hub/adhd/10-calming-and-regulating-activities-for-adhd

22. Carter, L. (2021, June 21). "You can't pour from an empty cup": why self-care isn't selfish. Modern Minds. https://modern-minds.com/you-cant-pour-from-an-empty-cup-why-self-care-isnt-selfish/

23. CDC. (2017, September 7). Trends in the parent-report of health care provider-diagnosis and medication treatment for ADHD. Centers for Disease Control and Prevention. https://www.cdc.gov/ncbddd/adhd/features/key-findings-adhd72013.html

24. CDC. (2019, August 27). Other concerns and conditions with ADHD. Centers for Disease Control and Prevention. https://www.cdc.gov/ncbddd/adhd/conditions.html

25. Centers for Disease Control and Prevention. (2022a). ADHD in the classroom. Centers for Disease Control and Prevention. https://www.cdc.gov/ncbddd/adhd/school-success.html

26. Centers for Disease Control and Prevention. (2022b, August 9). Data and statistics about ADHD. Centers for Disease Control and Prevention. https://www.cdc.gov/ncbddd/adhd/data.html

27. Centers for Disease Control and Prevention. (2022c, August 9). Symptoms and diagnosis of ADHD. Centers for Disease Control and Prevention. https://www.cdc.gov/ncbddd/adhd/diagnosis.html

28. CHADD. (2018a). About ADHD - symptoms, causes and treatment. CHADD. https://chadd.org/about-adhd/overview/

29. CHADD. (2018b). Coexisting conditions. CHADD. [https://chadd.org/about-

adhd/coexisting-conditions/](https://chadd.org/about-adhd/coexisting-conditions/)

30. CHADD. (2018c). General prevalence of ADHD. CHADD. https://chadd.org/about-adhd/general-prevalence/

31. CHADD's ADHD parents together. (n.d.). HealthUnlocked. https://healthunlocked.com/adhd-parents

32. Cherry, K. (2022, June 23). How to find an ADHD support group. Verywell Mind. https://www.verywellmind.com/how-to-find-an-adhd-support-group-5324827

33. Cherry, K. (2023, May 2). Emotional intelligence: how we perceive, evaluate, express, and control emotions. Verywell Mind. https://www.verywellmind.com/what-is-emotional-intelligence-2795423

34. Child ADHD testing benefits. (2023, June 12). Behavioral Health Clinic | Counseling & Therapy in Central Wisconsin. https://wibehavioralhealth.com/benefits-of-adhd-testing-for-your-child/

35. Children and adolescents | ADHD assessments. (2023). Adhdcare. https://www.adhdcare.co.uk/?p=children.and.adolescents

36. Chronister, D. K., Program, K. H. T. T., & Program, D. K. C. and K. H. T. T. (2021, June 19). Best activities for teens with ADHD - Key healthcare. Key Healthcare. https://keyhealthcare.com/activities-for-teens-with-adhd/

37. Clatch, M. PsyD. (2014, December 4). Is art therapy for ADHD the right choice for your child? Good Therapy Therapy Blog. https://www.goodtherapy.org/blog/is-art-therapy-for-adhd-the-right-choice-for-your-child-1204144

38. Cronkleton, E. (2019, April 9). 10 breathing techniques. Healthline. https://www.healthline.com/health/breathing-exercise

39. Cuncic, A. (2019). Chill out: how to use progressive muscle relaxation to quell anxiety. Verywell Mind. https://www.verywellmind.com/how-do-i-practice-progressive-muscle-relaxation-3024400

40. Dave, U. P., Dingankar, S. R., Saxena, V. S., Joseph, J. A., Bethapudi, B., Agarwal, A., & Kudiganti, V. (2014). An open-label study to elucidate the effects of stan-

dardized Bacopa monnieri extract in the management of symptoms of attention-deficit hyperactivity disorder in children. Advances in Mind-Body Medicine, 28(2), 10–15. https://pubmed.ncbi.nlm.nih.gov/24682000/

41. Dolin, A. (2019, August 22). ADHD homework helper: 13 easy study skills. ADDitude. https://www.additudemag.com/homework-helper-adhd-study-skills/

42. Dvořáková, M., Sivoňová, M., Trebatická, J., Škodáček, I., Waczuliková, I., Muchová, J., & Ďuračková, Z. (2006). The effect of polyphenolic extract from pine bark, Pycnogenol® on the level of glutathione in children suffering from attention deficit hyperactivity disorder (ADHD). Redox Report, 11(4), 163–172. https://doi.org/10.1179/135100006x116664

43. Einstein, A. (2023). Albert Einstein quotes. Goodreads. https://www.goodreads.com/quotes/8136665-everybody-is-a-genius-but-if-you-judge-a-fish

44. Elmaghraby, R., & Garayalde, S. (2022, June). What is ADHD? Psychiatry. https://www.psychiatry.org/patients-families/adhd/what-is-adhd

45. Emotional intelligence and ADHD. (2018, May 24). Cameron Gott. https://www.camerongott.com/blog/2018/05/24/emotional-intelligence-adhd

46. Every child with ADHD symptoms needs a hobby – here's why. (2018, June 3). The ADHD Centre. https://www.adhdcentre.co.uk/every-child-with-adhd-symptoms-needs-a-hobby-heres-why/

47. Faster Than Normal. (2021, January 27). ADHD and STEM w/ Raven the Science Maven, Dr. Raven Baxter. Faster than Normal. https://www.fasterthannormal.com/adhd-and-stem-w-raven-the-science-maven-dr-raven-baxter/

48. Flannery, S. (2023). What we know about ADHD and food. Child Mind Institute. https://childmind.org/article/what-we-know-about-adhd-and-food/

49. Forry, E. (2023, March 2). 22 super helpful apps for kids with ADHD - FamilyEducation. Family Education. [https://www.familyeducation.com/kids/neurodiversity/adhd/22-super-helpful-apps-for-kids-with-adhd#toc-time-management-apps-for-kids](https://www.familyeducation.com/kids/neurodi

versity/adhd/22-super-helpful-apps-for-kids-with-adhd#toc-time-manage ment-apps-for-kids)

50. Geisel, T. S. (n.d.). Dr. Seuss quotes. Goodreads. [https://www.goodreads.com/ quotes/16373-you-re-off-to-great-places-today-is-your-day-your](https:// www.goodreads.com/quotes/16373-you-re-off-to-great-places-today-is-your- day-your)

Continuing the APA format references:

51. Getahun, D., Rhoads, G. G., Demissie, K., Lu, S.-E., Quinn, V. P., Fassett, M. J., Wing, D. A., & Jacobsen, S. J. (2012). In-utero exposure to Ischemic-Hypoxic conditions and Attention-Deficit/Hyperactivity Disorder. Pediatrics, 131(1), e53–e61. [https://doi.org/10.1542/peds.2012-1298](https://doi.org/10.1542/ peds.2012-1298)

52. Glasser, J. M. (2020, August). Calming down and cooling off. CHADD. [https:// chadd.org/attention-article/calming-down-and-cooling-off/](https://chadd. org/attention-article/calming-down-and-cooling-off/)

53. Gratitude quotes (1708 quotes). (2009). Goodreads. [https://www.goodreads. com/quotes/tag/gratitude](https://www.goodreads.com/quotes/tag/gratitude)

54. Griffin, R. M. (2022, January 23). Ways to study better. WebMD. [https://www. webmd.com/add-adhd/childhood-adhd/study-better](https://www.webmd. com/add-adhd/childhood-adhd/study-better)

55. Haan, E., Westmoreland, K. E., Schellhas, L., Sallis, H. M., Taylor, G., Zuccolo, L., & Munafò, M. R. (2022). Prenatal smoking, alcohol and caffeine exposure and offspring externalizing disorders: a systematic review and meta-analysis. Addiction. [https://doi.org/10.1111/add.15858](https://doi.org/10.1111/add. 15858)

56. Han, J.-Y., Kwon, H.-J., Ha, M., Paik, K.-C., Lim, M.-H., Gyu Lee, S., Yoo, S.-J., & Kim, E.-J. (2015). The effects of prenatal exposure to alcohol and environmental tobacco smoke on risk for ADHD: A large population-based study. Psychiatry Research, 225(1-2), 164–168. [https://doi.org/10.1016/j.psychres.2014.11.009] (https://doi.org/10.1016/j.psychres.2014.11.009)

57. Harkin, C. (2019, May 13). Attention Deficit Hyperactivity Disorder and Play Therapy. Play Therapy Melbourne. [https://www.playtherapymelbourne.com/ attention-deficit-hyperactivity-disorder-and-play-therapy/](https://www. playtherapymelbourne.com/attention-deficit-hyperactivity-disorder-and-play- therapy/)

58. Herndon, J. (2021, April 13). ADHD medication side effects: What to know. Healthline. https://www.healthline.com/health/adhd/adhd-medication-side- effects

59. Hillman, C. H., Pontifex, M. B., Castelli, D. M., Khan, N. A., Raine, L. B.,

Scudder, M. R., Drollette, E. S., Moore, R. D., Wu, C.-T., & Kamijo, K. (2014). Effects of the FITKids randomized controlled trial on executive control and brain function. Pediatrics, 134(4), e1063–e1071. https://doi.org/10.1542/peds.2013-3219

60. Hiscock, H., Sciberras, E., Mensah, F., Gerner, B., Efron, D., Khano, S., & Oberklaid, F. (2015). Impact of a behavioural sleep intervention on symptoms and sleep in children with attention deficit hyperactivity disorder, and parental mental health: randomised controlled trial. BMJ, 350(jan20 1), h68–h68. https://doi.org/10.1136/bmj.h68

Continuing the APA format references:

61. Hoogman, M., Bralten, J., Hibar, D. P., Mennes, M., Zwiers, M. P., Schweren, L. S. J., van Hulzen, K. J. E., Medland, S. E., Shumskaya, E., Jahanshad, N., Zeeuw, P. de, Szekely, E., Sudre, G., Wolfers, T., Onnink, A. M. H., Dammers, J. T., Mostert, J. C., Vives-Gilabert, Y., Kohls, G., & Oberwelland, E. (2017). Subcortical brain volume differences in participants with attention deficit hyperactivity disorder in children and adults: a cross-sectional mega-analysis. The Lancet. Psychiatry, 4(4), 310–319. https://doi.org/10.1016/S2215-0366(17)30049-4

62. Howard, A. L., Robinson, M., Smith, G. J., Ambrosini, G. L., Piek, J. P., & Oddy, W. H. (2010). ADHD is associated with a "Western" dietary pattern in adolescents. Journal of Attention Disorders, 15(5), 403–411. https://doi.org/10.1177/1087054710365990

63. Hoza, B., Smith, A. L., Shoulberg, E. K., Linnea, K. S., Dorsch, T. E., Blazo, J. A., Alerding, C. M., & McCabe, G. P. (2014). A randomized trial examining the effects of aerobic physical activity on Attention-Deficit/Hyperactivity Disorder symptoms in young children. Journal of Abnormal Child Psychology, 43(4), 655–667. https://doi.org/10.1007/s10802-014-9929-y

64. Hsu, C., Hsieh, L., Chen, Y., Lin, I., Chen, Y., Chen, C., Shirakawa, H., & Yang, S. (2021). Complementary effects of pine bark extract supplementation on inattention, impulsivity, and antioxidative status in children with attention-deficit hyperactivity disorder: a double-blinded randomized placebo-controlled crossover study. Phytotherapy Research, doi: 10.1002/ptr.7036. https://doi.org/10.1002/ptr.7036

65. Hughes, L. (2023, May 24). ADHD productivity hack: how to use the Pomodoro method to get things done. Getinflow. https://www.getinflow.io/post/pomodoro-technique-adhd-productivity

66. I suffer OCD and ADD, Timberlake confesses. (2009, January 31). Stuff.

https://www.stuff.co.nz/entertainment/504629/I-suffer-OCD-and-ADD-Timberlake-confesses

67. Intentional Living. (n.d.). 7 different ways to journal. The Beautiful Life Plan. https://www.thebeautifullifeplan.com/blog/7-different-ways-to-journal] (https://www.thebeautifullifeplan.com/blog/7-different-ways-to-journal)

68. Jackson, N. A. (2003). A survey of music therapy methods and their role in the treatment of early elementary school children with ADHD. Journal of Music Therapy, 40(4), 302–323. https://doi.org/10.1093/jmt/40.4.302

69. Jones, H. (2022, January 17). Do ADHD symptoms differ in boys and girls? Verywell Health. https://www.verywellhealth.com/do-adhd-symptoms-differ-in-boys-and-girls-5207995

70. Jones, R. (2023, May 2). 51 inspirational breathe quotes to help find your center. Happier Human. [https://www.happierhuman.com/breathe-quotes-rj1/] (https://www.happierhuman.com/breathe-quotes-rj1/)

71. Jones, T. W., Borg, W. P., Boulware, S. D., McCarthy, G., Sherwin, R. S., & Tamborlane, W. V. (1995). Enhanced adrenomedullary response and increased susceptibility to neuroglycopenia: mechanisms underlying the adverse effects of sugar ingestion in healthy children. The Journal of Pediatrics, 126(2), 171–177. https://doi.org/10.1016/s0022-3476(95)70541-4

72. Journey of life quotes (455 quotes). (2023). Goodreads. https://www.goodreads.com/quotes/tag/journey-of-life

73. Karp, Dr. H. (2023). How to help your child with ADHD sleep better. Happiest Baby. https://www.happiestbaby.com/blogs/toddler/adhd-and-sleep

74. Kingsolver, B. (n.d.). Barbara Kingsolver quotes. Goodreads. https://www.goodreads.com/quotes/9156587-all-the-noise-in-my-brain-i-clamp-it-to

75. Knost, L. R. (n.d.) L. R. Knost quotes. Goodreads. [https://www.goodreads.com/quotes/9180745-taking-care-of-myself-doesn-t-mean-me-first-it-means] (https://www.goodreads.com/quotes/9180745-taking-care-of-myself-doesn-t-mean-me-first-it-means)

76. Kreider, C. M., Medina, S., & Slamka, M. R. (2019). Strategies for coping with time-related and productivity challenges of young people with learning disabili-

ties and Attention-Deficit/Hyperactivity Disorder. Children, 6(2), 28. https://doi.org/10.3390/children6020028

77. Kristenson, S. (2022, September 21). 7 5-minute mindfulness activities to quickly calm yourself. Happier Human. https://www.happierhuman.com/5-minute-mindfulness-activities/

78. Learning Disabilities Association of America. (2019). https://ldaamerica.org/

79. Lee, J., Lee, A., Kim, J.-H., Shin, Y. M., Kim, S.-J., Cho, W. D., & Lee, S. I. (2020). Effect of Omega-3 and Korean Red Ginseng on children with Attention Deficit Hyperactivity Disorder: an open-label pilot study. Clinical Psychopharmacology and Neuroscience, 18(1), 75–80. https://doi.org/10.9758/cpn.2020.18.1.75

80. Lee, S.-H., Park, W.-S., & Lim, M.-H. (2011). Clinical effects of Korean Red Ginseng on Attention Deficit Hyperactivity Disorder in children: an observational study. Journal of Ginseng Research, 35(2), 226–234. https://doi.org/10.5142/jgr.2011.35.2.226

81. Lesser, J. (2022, June 14). Sibling rivalry: ADHD family dynamics, positive parenting & more. ADDitude. https://www.additudemag.com/sibling-rivalry-adhd-positive-parenting-tips/

82. Lingasubramanian, G., Corman, H., Noonan, K., & Reichman, N. E. (2022, August 5). Linkinghub. Elsevier. https://linkinghub.elsevier.com/retrieve/pii/S0022347622006989

83. Logan, A. (2022, December 6). Can expressing gratitude improve health? Mayo Clinic Health System. https://www.mayoclinichealthsystem.org/hometown-health/speaking-of-health/can-expressing-gratitude-improve-health

84. Lovering, N. (2022, February 21). Cognitive Behavioral Therapy for ADHD: How can it help? Psych Central. https://psychcentral.com/adhd/cbt-for-adhd

85. Lugo-Candelas, C., Corbeil, T., Wall, M., Posner, J., Bird, H., Canino, G., Fisher, P. W., Suglia, S. F., & Duarte, C. S. (2020). ADHD and risk for subsequent adverse childhood experiences: understanding the cycle of adversity. Journal of Child Psychology and Psychiatry, 62(8). https://doi.org/10.1111/jcpp.13352

86. McCarthy, L. F. (2006, November 30). ADHD medications for children.

ADDitude. [https://www.additudemag.com/adhd-medications-for-children/] (https://www.additudemag.com/adhd-medications-for-children/)

87. Miller, G. (2019, October 23). ADHD resources: support groups, books, apps, and more. Psych Central. [https://psychcentral.com/adhd/adhd-resources#take away](https://psychcentral.com/adhd/adhd-resources#takeaway)

88. Morin, A. (2019). The 8 most effective ways to discipline a child with ADHD. Verywell Family. [https://www.verywellfamily.com/discipline-strategies-for-kids-with-adhd-1094941](https://www.verywellfamily.com/discipline-strate gies-for-kids-with-adhd-1094941)

89. Morin, A. (n.d.). 8 common myths about ADHD. Understood. [https://www. understood.org/en/articles/common-myths-about-adhd](https://www.under stood.org/en/articles/common-myths-about-adhd)

90. Moryoussef, K. (2022, February 14). "How I calm down my ADHD brain: 14 quick de-stressors." ADDitude. https://www.additudemag.com/how-to-calm-down-destress-techniques-adhd/

91. Moser, J. S., Schroder, H. S., Heeter, C., Moran, T. P., & Lee, Y.-H. (2011). Mind your errors: Evidence for a neural mechanism linking growth mind-set to adaptive posterror adjustments. Psychological Science, 22(12), 1484–1489. [https:// doi.org/10.1177/0956797611419520](https://doi.org/10.1177/ 0956797611419520)

92. Myers, P. (2022, February 7). Communication strategies for parents of children with ADHD. Child Development Institute. [https://childdevelopmentinfo.com/ parenting/communication-strategies-parents-children-adhd/](https://childde velopmentinfo.com/parenting/communication-strategies-parents-children-adhd/)

93. Narad, M. E., Kennelly, M., Zhang, N., Wade, S. L., Yeates, K. O., Taylor, H. G., Epstein, J. N., & Kurowski, B. G. (2018). Secondary Attention-Deficit/Hyperactivity Disorder in children and adolescents 5 to 10 years after traumatic brain injury. JAMA Pediatrics, 172(5), 437–443. [https://doi.org/10. 1001/jamapediatrics.2017.5746](https://doi.org/10.1001/jamapediatrics. 2017.5746)

94. Nelson, W. (2006, October 6). "Why couldn't he be like any other boy?" ADDitude. [https://www.additudemag.com/adhd-personal-stories/](https:// www.additudemag.com/adhd-personal-stories/)

95. Next Step 4 ADHD. (2021, February 8). 6 indoor exercise ideas for kids with ADHD. Next Step 4 ADHD. https://nextstep4adhd.com/6-indoor-exercise-ideas-for-kids-with-adhd/

96. Nigg, J. T., & Holton, K. (2014). Restriction and elimination diets in ADHD

treatment. Child and Adolescent Psychiatric Clinics of North America, 23(4), 937–953. https://doi.org/10.1016/j.chc.2014.05.010

97. Novotni, M. (2021, May 13). Can't take him anywhere. ADDitude. https://www.additudemag.com/cant-take-him-anywhere/

98. Novotni, M., & Ph.D. (2007, July 10). No judgment. No guilt. Just ADHD support and understanding. ADDitude. https://www.additudemag.com/youre-not-alone/

99. Oh, the Places You'll Go! (2023). Goodreads. https://www.goodreads.com/quotes/16373-you-re-off-to-great-places-today-is-your-day-your

100. 101 anxiety quotes to help you get through and lift your spirits. (2020, February 1). Parade. https://parade.com/951718/parade/anxiety-quotes/

101. Ovcharenko, J. (2023, November 2). I have no patience for my ADHD child! Tips and hacks. Numo. https://numo.so/journal/i-have-no-patience-for-my-adhd-child

102. Pahwa, V. (2023, March 30). 60 insane fill your cup quotes to rehydrate your life. Uprisehigh. https://uprisehigh.com/simplify-life/fill-your-cup-quotes/

103. Parenting teenagers with ADHD. (2023). HealthyChildren. https://www.healthychildren.org/English/health-issues/conditions/adhd/Pages/Effective-Parenting-of-Teenagers-with-ADHD.aspx

104. Phillips, H. (2021, October 22). 6 essential time management practices for kids & teens with ADHD. Exceptional Mindset. https://www.exceptionalmindset.org/post/6-essential-time-management-practices-for-kids-teens-with-adhd

105. Positive affirmation quotes (336 quotes). (2023). Goodreads. https://www.goodreads.com/quotes/tag/positive-affirmation

106. Practicing deep breathing for better physical and mental health. (2023, March 28). One step. https://www.onestep.co/resources-blog/deep-breathing-better-physical-mental-health

107. Pros and cons of ADHD medication. (2010, July). Consumer Reports. https://www.consumerreports.org/cro/2013/01/the-pros-and-cons-of-treating-adhd-with-drugs/index.htm

108. Proust, M. (n.d.). Marcel Proust quotes. Brainy Quote. https://www.brainyquote.com/quotes/marcel_proust_105251

109. Ptacek, R., Weissenberger, S., Braaten, E., Klicperova-Baker, M., Goetz, M., Raboch, J., Vnukova, M., & Stefano, G. B. (2019). Clinical implications of the perception of time in Attention Deficit Hyperactivity Disorder (ADHD): a review. Medical Science Monitor, 25, 3918–3924. https://doi.org/10.12659/msm.914225

110. Rapaport, L. (2017, December 18). Preemies and underweight babies more likely to develop ADHD. Reuters. https://www.reuters.com/article/us-health-adhd-preterm-underweight-idUSKBN1EC2P5/

111. Raymond, J. (2022, May 28). ADHD stigma in children and teens. WebMD. https://www.webmd.com/add-adhd/childhood-adhd/adhd-stigma-children-teens

112. Rees, M. (2023, June 2). ADHD time management tips and suggestions. Medical News Today. https://www.medicalnewstoday.com/articles/adhd-time-management

113. Relaxation techniques: breath control helps quell errant stress responses. (2020, July 6). Harvard Health. https://www.health.harvard.edu/mind-and-mood/relaxation-techniques-breath-control-helps-quell-errant-stress-response

114. Rubia, K. (2018). Cognitive neuroscience of Attention Deficit Hyperactivity Disorder (ADHD) and its clinical translation. Frontiers in Human Neuroscience, 12(100). https://doi.org/10.3389/fnhum.2018.00100

115. Saline, S., & Psy.D. (2021, June 13). When ADHD drains and strains sibling relationships. ADDitude. https://www.additudemag.com/sibling-relationships-adhd-families/

116. Sarris, J., Kean, J., Schweitzer, I., & Lake, J. (2011). Complementary medicines (herbal and nutritional products) in the treatment of Attention Deficit Hyperactivity Disorder (ADHD): a systematic review of the evidence.

Complementary Therapies in Medicine, 19(4), 216–227. https://doi.org/10.1016/j.ctim.2011.06.007

117. Sauber Millacci, T. (2021, December 29). How to nurture a growth mindset in kids: 8 best activities. Positive Psychology. https://positivepsychology.com/growth-mindset-for-kids/#definition

118. Schein, J., Adler, L. A., Childress, A., Gagnon-Sanschagrin, P., Davidson, M., Kinkead, F., Cloutier, M., Guérin, A., & Lefebvre, P. (2022). Economic burden of attention-deficit/hyperactivity disorder among adults in the United States: a societal perspective. Journal of Managed Care & Specialty Pharmacy, 28(2), 168–179. https://doi.org/10.18553/jmcp.2021.21290

119. Sciberras, E., Efron, D., Patel, P., Mulraney, M., Lee, K. J., Mihalopoulos, C., Engel, L., Rapee, R. M., Anderson, V., Nicholson, J. M., Schembri, R., & Hiscock, H. (2019). Does the treatment of anxiety in children with Attention-Deficit/Hyperactivity Disorder (ADHD) using cognitive behavioral therapy improve child and family outcomes? Protocol for a randomized controlled trial. BMC Psychiatry, 19(1). https://doi.org/10.1186/s12888-019-2276-3

120. Self-Care for parents of kids with behavioral challenges. (2023). Brain Balance Centers. https://www.brainbalancecenters.com/blog/self-care-behavioral-challenges

Continuing the APA format references:

121. Sharon. (2021, November 17). ADHD, emotional regulation and managing family conflict: replacing time-outs with time-in or time-apart. Dr. Sharon Saline. https://drsharonsaline.com/2021/11/16/adhd-emotional-regulation-and-managing-family-conflict-replacing-time-outs-with-time-in-or-time-apart/

122. Sharpe, R. (2021, February 12). 150+ mindfulness quotes to help you live more mindfully. Declutter the Mind. https://declutterthemind.com/blog/mindfulness-quotes/

123. Simone Biles - Sport star acknowledged her diagnosis of ADHD. (2022, August 13). Adhduk. https://adhduk.co.uk/2022/08/13/simone-biles/

124. Singhal, M. (2021). 6 things emotionally intelligent parents do differently. Psychology Today. [https://www.psychologytoday.com/intl/blog/the-therapist-mommy/202101/6-things-emotionally-intelligent-parents-do-differently]

(https://www.psychologytoday.com/intl/blog/the-therapist-mommy/202101/6-things-emotionally-intelligent-parents-do-differently)

125. 6 ways to improve communication with kids with ADHD. (2021, February 22). The ADHD Centre. https://www.adhdcentre.co.uk/6-ways-to-improve-communication-with-kids-with-adhd/

126. Sleep program helping ADHD kids rest easier and improve quality of life. (2019, January 22). Murdoch Children's Research Institute. https://www.mcri.edu.au/news-stories/sleep-program-helping-adhd-kids-rest-easier-and-improve-quality-life

127. Smith, M. (2019). HelpGuide.org. https://www.helpguide.org/articles/add-adhd/attention-deficit-disorder-adhd-and-school.htm

128. Song, P., Zha, M., Yang, Q., Zhang, Y., Li, X., & Rudan, I. (2021). The prevalence of adult attention-deficit hyperactivity disorder: a global systematic review and meta-analysis. Journal of Global Health, 11(04009). https://doi.org/10.7189/jogh.11.04009

129. Spurgeon, C. (n.d.). Charles Spurgeon quotes. Brainy Quote. https://www.brainyquote.com/quotes/charles_spurgeon_132220

130. Steck, J. T. (2017, September 6). Fostering resilience and grit in those with ADHD. Children's Resource Group. https://www.childrensresourcegroup.com/fostering-resilience-and-grit-in-those-with-adhd/

131. Steele, C. M. (1988). The psychology of self-affirmation: sustaining the integrity of the self. Advances in Experimental Social Psychology, 21, 261–302. https://doi.org/10.1016/s0065-2601(08)60229-4

132. Stessman, E. (2023, May 3). Can journaling help relieve stress? Experts weigh in on the benefits. Today. https://www.today.com/shop/how-journal-mental-health-benefits-t255576

133. Story, C. M. (2017, September 22). These 6 herbs may help treat ADHD. Healthline. https://www.healthline.com/health/adhd/herbal-remedies#ginkgo-biloba

134. Strahm, C. D. (2020). Parents' experience raising a child with Attention Deficit Hyperactivity Disorder (ADHD). Sigma Repository. [https://sigma.nursingrepository.org/handle/10755/19351](https://sigma.nursingrepository.org/handle/

10755/19351)

135. Tariq, O. (2022, May 31). Stimulant vs non stimulant ADHD meds: key differences. Breining. https://www.breining.edu/wp-content/uploads/2015/08/JAD15SFG.pdf

136. Taylor-Klaus, E. (2021, September 6). 10 Tips to improve communication with your ADHD child's teachers. Impactparents. https://impactparents.com/blog/adhd/tips-to-improve-communication-with-your-childs-teacher/

137. Tewari, A. (2022, August 21). The joy of a gratitude jar and how to make it today. Gratitude - the Life Blog. https://blog.gratefulness.me/gratitude-jar/

138. The Understood Team. (n.d.). How Michael Phelps' ADHD helped him make Olympic history. Understood. https://www.understood.org/en/articles/celebrity-spotlight-how-michael-phelps-adhd-helped-him-make-olympic-history

139. Therapy for ADHD (for Parents). (2017). Kidshealth.org. https://kidshealth.org/en/parents/adhd-therapy.html

140. Thompson, C. (2023). The power of yet: growth mindset | Beyond the Classroom. Beyond the Classroom. https://beyondtheclassroom.ca/the-power-of-yet-growth-mindset/

141. Time management for parents - 14 tips for better family time. (n.d.). Time Management Success. https://www.time-management-success.com/time-management-for-parents.html

142. Timer, Online Countdown. (n.d.). Online bomb timer. Online-Stopwatch. https://www.online-stopwatch.com/bomb-countdown/

143. Tolle, E. (n.d.). Eckhart Tolle quotes. Brainy Quote. https://www.brainyquote.com/quotes/eckhart_tolle_571595

144. Trebatická, J., Kopasová, S., Hradečná, Z., Činovský, K., Škodáček, I., Šuba, J., Muchová, J., Žitňanová, I., Waczulíková, I., Rohdewald, P., & Ďuračková, Z. (2006). Treatment of ADHD with French maritime pine bark extract, Pycnogenol®. European Child & Adolescent Psychiatry, 15(6), 329–335. [https://doi.org/10.1007/s00787-006-0538-3](https://doi.org/10.1007/

s00787-006-0538-3)

145. Tucker, G. C. (n.d.-a). Astronaut Scott Kelly opens up about ADHD. Understood. https://www.understood.org/en/articles/astronaut-scott-kelly-opens-up-about-his-attention-issues

146. Tucker, G. C. (n.d.-b). Channing Tatum on his ADHD and dyslexia | In the News. Understood. https://www.understood.org/en/articles/channing-tatum-on-his-adhd-and-dyslexia

147. 20 journaling prompts for mental health. (2022, November 30). Mindful Health Solutions. https://mindfulhealthsolutions.com/20-journaling-prompts-for-mental-health/

148. Volkow, N. D., Wang, G.-J., Kollins, S. H., Wigal, T. L., Newcorn, J. H., Telang, F., Fowler, J. S., Zhu, W., Logan, J., Ma, Y., Pradhan, K., Wong, C., & Swanson, J. M. (2009). Evaluating dopamine reward pathway in ADHD. JAMA, 302(10), 1084. https://doi.org/10.1001/jama.2009.1308

149. Walt Disney: ADHD and dyslexia. (2023). Studymode. https://www.studymode.com/essays/Walt-Disney-ADHD-And-Dyslexia-8B08977007A6E106.html

150. Walt, M. (2015, May 12). How to recognize ADHD symptoms at every age. WebMD. https://www.webmd.com/add-adhd/childhood-adhd/features/adhd-symptoms-age

151. WebMD Editorial Contributors. (2023, April 18). ADHD Behavioral Therapy for Kids. WebMD. https://www.webmd.com/add-adhd/childhood-adhd/adhd-behavioral-treatment

152. Who can diagnose ADHD. (2023, January 21). ADHD-BED Integrated. https://adhd.clinic/news-research/who-can-diagnose-adhd/

153. Wilde, E. M., & Welch, G. F. (2022). Attention deficit hyperactivity disorder (ADHD) and musical behavior: The significance of context. Psychology of Music, 50(6), 030573562210811. https://doi.org/10.1177/03057356221081163

154. Williams, Y. (2021, May 29). Ten ways parents can be more effective using emotional intelligence. The Guardian Nigeria News. [https://guardian.ng/guardian-woman/ten-ways-parents-can-be-more-effective-using-emotional-

intelligence/](https://guardian.ng/guardian-woman/ten-ways-parents-can-be-more-effective-using-emotional-intelligence/)

155. Wirth, J. (2023, June 6). ADHD statistics and facts in 2023. Forbes Health. https://www.forbes.com/health/mind/adhd-statistics/

156. Wright, K. W. (2023, February 10). 100+ quotes about journaling. Day One | Your Journal for Life. https://dayoneapp.com/blog/quotes-about-journaling/

157. Yu, C.-J., Du, J.-C., Chiou, H.-C., Chung, M.-Y., Yang, W., Chen, Y.-S., Fuh, M.-R., Chien, L.-C., Hwang, B., & Chen, M.-L. (2016). Increased risk of attention-deficit/hyperactivity disorder associated with exposure to organophosphate pesticide in Taiwanese children. Andrology, 4(4), 695–705. https://doi.org/10.1111/andr.12183

158. Zhang, T., Sidorchuk, A., Sevilla-Cermeño, L., Vilaplana-Pérez, A., Chang, Z., Larsson, H., Mataix-Cols, D., & Fernández de la Cruz, L. (2019). Association of Cesarean delivery with risk of neurodevelopmental and psychiatric disorders in the offspring. JAMA Network Open, 2(8), e1910236. https://doi.org/10.1001/jamanetworkopen.2019.10236